1781:
The Battle of Jersey and
The Death of Major Peirson

1781:
The Battle of Jersey and
The Death of Major Peirson

Louise Downie and Doug Ford

First published Jersey 2012

by Jersey Heritage
Text copyright © Jersey Heritage
Illustrations © individuals and
organisations credited

Front cover: *The Death of Major Peirson*, 1783
by John Singleton Copley, © Tate, London 2011
(N00733)

ISBN 978-0-9562079-7-5

Jersey
Heritage

Contents

Foreword

The image of the Battle of Jersey created by John Singleton Copley is so familiar to Islanders. It has over the years been reproduced on items as diverse as telephone directories, banknotes and postage stamps. Those small reproductions however do not create the impact of the original canvas. I well remember being taken as a child to the Tate Gallery in London to see the original painting and being so impressed by the sensation of the fierce Battle that this large scale work conveys.

The Battle itself was of course an important point in the Island's history. What a different Island this would be in terms of society, economy and landscape but for the bravery and sacrifice of Major Peirson and his men?

I write this foreword as I sit in Benest & Syvret's offices at 16 Hill Street, a building which was constructed in 1742. My office now looks out onto the States' building, but at the time of the Battle the window from my office would have provided a clear view of the desperate fighting. Our firm's building is believed to be one of the buildings which form the backdrop to Copley's painting.

Benest & Syvret are delighted to be co-sponsoring the exhibition of *The Death of Major Peirson* in Jersey. It will provide a ready opportunity for all Islanders to learn more about the painting and the Battle as an important part of Island history. I hope that the painting will have an equal impact on the schoolchildren who come to the exhibition as it had on me all those years ago.

Philip Syvret
Benest & Syvret Advocates and Solicitors

 Spearpoint

 hepburns insurance

 INSURANCE CORPORATION

 Camerons

 Benest &Syvret

Acknowledgements

This publication has been produced in association with the exhibition of the same title - *1781: The Battle of Jersey and The Death of Major Peirson*. This project would not have been possible without the help of several organisations and individuals to whom Jersey Heritage is immensely grateful. Tate have not only loaned Jersey Heritage the painting *The Death of Major Peirson* 1783 by John Singleton Copley, their staff have provided tremendous support and help. The Courtauld Gallery have loaned Jersey Heritage sketches for the painting providing an invaluable insight into the artist's thought processes and artistic practice and again Jersey Heritage are grateful not only for these loans but for the help and advice throughout the process.

Each of the project sponsors and supporters has made a unique contribution to the *1781: The Battle of Jersey and The Death of Major Peirson* project, but all have in common their unstinting enthusiasm for bringing *The Death of Major Peirson* to Jersey for the first time.

Thanks to Spearpoint Limited for their generous sponsorship at the eleventh hour. Hepburns Insurance and Insurance Corporation of the Channel Islands have provided invaluable support, flexibility and advice. Camerons Ltd has been committed to this project from its inception and their positive 'can do' attitude has calmed the worries of a nervous curator! Sir Philip Bailhache has been unflagging in his efforts to raise money to enable this project and was successful in gathering an army of supporters - Pam and Paul Bell, Advocate Alan Binnington, Advocate Graham Boxall, Lord Brownlow, Advocate Jonathan Speck and The 42 Foundation - as well as making a contribution on behalf of himself and Lady Bailhache. Sir Philip and Rosy Dessain should also be thanked for facilitating the sponsorship of this publication by Benest & Syvret, whose enthusiasm for this project is manifest in their foreword.

Many organisations have allowed Jersey Heritage to reproduce images from their collections in this publication and Jersey Heritage would like to acknowledge contributions from: Tate, London; The Samuel Courtauld Trust, The Courtauld Gallery, London; Museum of Fine Arts, Boston; Yale University Art Gallery; Metropolitan Museum of Art, New York; Sir John Soane's Museum; The Library of Congress; The National Gallery of Canada, Ottawa; Victoria & Albert Museum, London; Imperial War Museum, La Société Jersiaise and Associated Press.

1781: The Battle of Jersey and The Death of Major Peirson project is the culmination of years of work by many people working for Jersey Heritage. Sincere thanks to all of those people - your hard work, persistence and support is deeply appreciated. The project has also benefited from the amazing knowledge of many people including Emily Ballew Neff, curator of American painting and sculpture at the Museum of Fine Arts, Houston, Anna Baghiani of the Lord Coutanche Library, Société Jersiaise, Mick Low, museum manager at the Highlanders' Museum, Dave Dorgan and Terry Underwood of the 1781 Jersey Militia. Thanks also to Roger Hills and Julia Coutanche for their weekend proofreading and designer Deborah Shead.

Introduction

The Death of Major Peirson, 1782 - 84 by John Singleton Copley (1738 - 1815) plucks at the heartstrings of the patriotic Jersey person. If it is true that a picture paints a thousand words then the words *The Death of Major Peirson* speaks are of years of conflict and aggression, of an Island struggling to maintain its allegiance to the British Crown and of one man's heroism and ultimate sacrifice. *The Death of Major Peirson* is indelibly linked to the Island's history. Because of its resonance as a visual archive of the Island's status, it has been reproduced countless times in the local newspaper, used in advertising, until recently was printed on Jersey money and there is a full-size copy in the Royal Court. Consequently most people in Jersey are familiar with the image, perhaps more than any other local work of art. But how did the artist go about creating a painting with such emotional and visual impact? Does it tell the truth? Why did he decide to paint this particular event rather than other things which were happening in the world at the time? Which bits of the story did he tell and which did he leave out? How did he exhibit and publicise the painting and how was it received by the public?

The Death of Major Peirson captures one moment during the events of 6 January 1781 and has come to symbolise the Battle of Jersey yet it tells us little of what actually happened on that day. In reality the Battle of Jersey was two separate relatively minor actions fought about five miles apart on the same day during the American Revolutionary War. What makes it unusual is that geographically it was fought on the wrong side of the Atlantic and, because it was a British victory over the French at a time of British military setbacks, it assumes a greater importance than would otherwise have been the case. The reports that have survived have tended to be from the Islanders' point of view and the role of the regular soldiers glossed over. Little has been said of why the Battle was fought in the way it was. This account seeks to address this and perhaps to launch a round of further enquiries into the period. However, there is still a lot to unravel before the true story of the Battle of Jersey is told.

The Battle of Jersey by Doug Ford

Jersey and France - hostile neighbours

The background to the Battle

Throughout the centuries the conflict between France and England has featured prominently in the history of Jersey. The origins of this conflict centre on the successful invasion of England by the Duke of Normandy, William the Conqueror in 1066. Jersey and the rest of the Channel Islands had become part of Normandy in 933 during the reign of the second duke, William I (Longsword). Following the Norman Conquest, the Islands were linked to the new English monarchy, through their allegiance to the Dukes of Normandy.

The consequence of this bond was to prove pivotal when, following the loss of Normandy to France by King John in 1204, the Channel Islands retained their allegiance to John. From their position as a peaceful backwater, the Islands became frontier posts on the edge of a war zone. Over the next 600 years the Islands were subjected to numerous attacks by the French culminating in the Battle of Jersey.

Following the British victory over the French and their allies in the Seven Years War (1756 - 63), the colonists in North America no longer had to fear a hostile European neighbour. Many colonists were frustrated by the limitations imposed upon their opportunities, caused by the British government's attempts to limit westward expansion to appease the French former Indian allies, and the conciliatory gestures made to the French Canadians through the 1774 Quebec Act. The cost of the Seven Years War had virtually bankrupted Britain and the King and his government saw the wealth of the expanded British world as a resource to be tapped into to claw back some of this debt. Freed of external threat, the American colonists embarked upon a course of political action that would eventually lead first of all to civil disobedience, then to civil conflict and finally to an all out war of independence.

Britain's enemies looked upon this escalating scenario as a great opportunity to retrieve some of the overseas possessions they had lost in 1763. France, Spain and Holland all provided clandestine support before the French came out openly in early 1778 and formed an alliance with the American secessionists fighting for independence. The alliance was to have an effect on the Atlantic trade that equally impacted on Jersey, which had longstanding trade links with America. Many of these links had been established over many years, from events such as the grant of land to Sir George Carteret by the English monarchy in the seventeenth century. The response to the alliance and the renewal of conflicts between England and France was to instigate a renewed period of privateering in the Channel Islands aimed at French shipping. The disruption this privateering activity caused brought about the expected demands for reprisals against the Island.

The clamour for retaliation against Jersey led to talks at the French court regarding the Island's capture. The initial attempt during this period was to be made by Charles Henry Otto of Nassau Siegen, the Prince of Nassau, an adventurer who had sailed around the world with the navigator and explorer Louis-Antoine, Comte de Bougainville (1729 - 1811).

He led his force of 1,500 men into St Malo on 19 April 1779 with the intention of sailing to Jersey the same day; however, adverse weather conditions forced them to camp on the island of Cézembre until the end of the month. On 30 April the men were loaded onto nearly 50 flat-bottomed boats of between four and 20 tons. The invasion flotilla, which was accompanied by five warships[1], was commanded by Captain de Chambertrand of the *Diana* and the spot chosen for the invasion was St Ouen's Bay. Despite being hampered by torrential rain and headwinds the fleet was in full view of St Aubin by 7.00am the following day. The alarm was raised and the 78th Highlanders, the Militia and units of the Royal Jersey Artillery were called out. The Lieutenant Governor, Major Moyse Corbet, in his own words described the event ...*from the heights above St Ouen's Bay, attending to the motions of the enemy: Jersey, May 1st, 1779, three o'clock in the afternoon. Early this morning five large vessels, and a great number of boats (which afterwards appeared to be French) were seen within three leagues of the coast, from whence they proceeded to St Ouen's Bay, in order, by a coup de main, to effect a landing. The cutters and small craft intended to cover their disembarkation, came so near as to throw some grape shot, and the boats were at hand to effect their purpose; but by the spirited march of the 78th, and the militia of the island with some few of the artillery of the island, which we were able to drag through the heavy sands, they were beat off, and obliged to give up their hostile intentions in that bay, without any loss on our side than a few men wounded by the bursting of a cannon; but the enemy remains within about a league of the coast, lying to, in order as we suppose, when the tide permits, to make a further attempt; in which case nothing shall be wanting on our part. The King's troops and militia have already gone through great fatigue, and show a spirit beyond my power to describe*[2].

During the brief engagement Corbet directed the troops. He had about 400 infantry and 40 mounted troopers deployed in a single rank along the length of the sand dunes. According to the *Gazette de L'Europe* of 7 May 1779, certain elements of the Prince of Nassau's army led by his second in command (who may have been Baron de Rullecourt) managed to land and issued a proclamation stating that the Island would form part of the Duchy of Normandy. Any further progress was prevented by the falling tide, a rising wind and stormy sea, forcing the warships to stand off leaving the landing craft unprotected, forcing them to retire as well and head back to St Malo.

The action resulted in the death of Thomas Picot when the cannon he was manning blew up and two sheep were killed by French cannon. There were some other casualties but no other fatalities as far as can be ascertained. Nassau's men retired once more to Cézembre and the transports and warships returned to Cancale to await further orders and another opportunity to attack Jersey.

Fearing they might return in the morning Corbet sat up all night in a St Lawrence guardhouse receiving reports from all over the Island. Before setting out to St Ouen, he had sent word to England that the Island was in need of help. The ship carrying the message met a British fleet sailing to America just off the Isle of Wight. As soon as Vice Admiral Marriot Arbuthnot got the message he changed course for the Island where he was joined by a further 13 ships sent from Portsmouth. On 12 May five frigates from this fleet carrying 134 cannon between them sailed for Cancale. Here they trapped the French warships in the roads on a falling tide, causing them to ground, whereupon the British ships opened up at point blank range and destroyed them. The *Valeur* of 48 cannon was burnt and the

Danae of 34 cannon was captured. Only two French ships managed to escape - the *Guepe*, a ten cannon cutter and *Ecluse*, a lighter carrying 20 cannon.

In the aftermath of the defeat of the French two years later *The London Gazette* whilst criticising the Governor, General Conway's absence from the Island at such a time did praise his preparation of the militia carried out the previous summer, *particularly as to the training and disciplining the militia, to which probably the island owes its present security*[3].

The military situation in Jersey

Fearing just such an invasion, General Conway had ordered the building of a series of defensive towers around the Island commanding the best landing sites. Combined with a great number of guardhouses, gun emplacements or batteries and accompanying powder houses manned by the Island militia, this building programme was intended to make the Island virtually impregnable. The regular troops manned the two main castles, Mont Orgueil and Elizabeth Castle, as well as sites like Fort Conway on Grouville Common.

Three line regiments had troops stationed in Jersey at the end of 1780. These were:
- five companies of Lord Seaforth's 78th Regiment of Foot (later to become the Seaforth Highlanders) - about 450 men;
- five companies[4] of Colonel Scott's 83rd Regiment of Foot (Royal Glasgow Volunteers) - about 390 men;
- all of Colonel Reid's 95th Regiment of Foot[5] - about 900 men;
- six companies of Invalids who manned the artillery in the forts - about 240 men; and
- a small number of Engineers commanded by Captain Mulcaster.

In addition to the regulars, the Island was defended by the Jersey Militia which was divided into five regiments

The Jerseymen treating y̆ French with Gunpowder Tea

Wood cut showing the defeat of the French landing in Jersey, 1779.

of Foot, a small regiment of cavalry and a corps of artillery with about 25 cannon. The parish churches were used to store equipment so that within two hours of the alarm being raised, over 2,500 fully armed militiamen could be at their predetermined positions. The effectiveness of this system can be gauged by the invasion scare of April 1793 when 17 French warships were sighted off the south coast, the St Helier battalion of the Fourth Regiment were at their posts within ten minutes of the alarm being raised. Although officially a volunteer force, service in the militia was compulsory for all British males between the ages of 17 and 65 normally resident in the Island.

The militia regiments were:

- 1st or North West Regiment from St Ouen, St Mary and St John
- 2nd or North Regiment from Trinity and St Martin
- 3rd or East Regiment from St Saviour, Grouville and St Clement
- 1/4th or South Regiment - St Helier Battalion drew men from Town
- 2/4th or South Regiment - St Lawrence Battalion drew men from that parish and the country parts of St Helier
- 5th or South West Regiment from St Peter and St Brelade

Major Francis Peirson, 1869
by P J Ouless (1817 - 85).
Jersey Heritage/Société Jersiaise Collection (SJA/1402)

Francis Peirson (1757 - 1781)

Major Francis Peirson was the eldest son of Francis Peirson and his wife Sarah Codgell of Mawthorpe in the East Riding of Yorkshire. Most contemporary records spell his name Pierson.

His military career began in 1772 when at the age of fifteen he was a commissioned ensign with the 36th Regiment of Foot of which his second cousin, Lieutenant General Sir Richard Peirson, was colonel. In August 1779 he was engaged to raise 100 men for the new 95th Regiment, which was to be raised in Yorkshire for the duration of the American Wars, and so was made a major[9]. He spent time recruiting in York until January 1780. As major he was third in command of the regiment and received 15/- per day of which 11/6 was deducted for subsistence. He was in sole command of the Regiment as it marched down to Plymouth.

The 95th arrived in Jersey in April 1780 and were stationed at La Hougue in St Peter.

It is interesting to note that even though Britain was in a state of war with France, both of his senior officers and those in the other regiments in the Island had returned to England for the Christmas period.

The Artillery Corps was divided into parish units and the men were attached to the Regiment in the area they lived.

Most regiments in the British army, both infantry and engineers[6], wore the standard 1768 uniform of close fitting, long tailed red coat, blue for artillery, with coloured facings (collars, cuffs and lapels), white waistcoat, white breeches and stockings with black gaiters, black shoes with buckles and a black cocked hat.[7]

The 78th Regiment would have been immediately recognisable as they were a Highland regiment and as such wore the kilt, diced hose, a short red coat with orange facings and a bonnet. As the 83rd was a Royal Regiment it was entitled to have royal blue 'facings' augmented by white lace on the button holes. The 95th Regiment also wore the standard 1768 uniform but with yellow facings. The Jersey Militia wore the same uniforms as the British army and each of the five regiments had their own facings.[8]

Preparing to invade

The idea of invading Jersey and diverting British resources from other areas of conflict persisted. Although not an 'official' expedition, de Rullecourt was charged with organising a fresh attempt on the Island which, should he succeed, would receive official sanction and rewards.

In December 1780 the Duke of Luxembourg, Baron de Rullecourt and M Vireau de Beauvoir met to finalise the details of attacking Jersey. Following this meeting, de Rullecourt made his way to Granville, the proposed embarkation point, where he met with Jean Regnier, tenant of Chaussey, who arranged for him to secretly cross over to Jersey to gain intelligence. Regnier was also in charge of organising the vessels needed to transport de Rullecourt's army over to Jersey. There were rumours of disgruntled Islanders helping the French and names were noted but there is no real evidence to support this accusation. One such person was Pierre Journeaux (1741 - 94) who was supposedly the man who piloted the French through the rocks and gullies at La Rocque. Despite the fact that he was supposed to be a traitor, he was never charged with treason and he continued to live in Jersey.

While de Rullecourt was gathering intelligence his Luxembourg Legion was held at Le Havre, far enough away from the Channel Islands to avoid suspicion. The Legion was being trained on a daily basis and received new men from all over France. By the time it left Le Havre on 19 December 1780 it had over 950 men in its ranks. It was a mixture of adventurers, amongst whom was Mir Saïd from southern India, convicts and soldiers drafted from other units. It took them eight days to march to Granville where, such was the suspicion of them, they were straight away embarked on 25 boats and taken to Chaussey. Here they were joined by three companies of militia from Lower Normandy and men from several provincial regiments, bringing the total up to about 1,200 men.

The weather delayed their plans for over a week. This was a crucial period for de Rullecourt as his great fear was that his men and accompanying fleet would be discovered by a patrolling Royal Navy vessel. Eventually on Friday, 5 January 1781 he was able to embark his men and at 3.00pm in the fading light of a winter's day, the French flotilla left Chaussey Sound bound for Jersey on the falling tide taking advantage of the tidal stream.

Philippe Charles Felix Macquart, Baron de Rullecourt
painted in 1780 by an unknown French artist.
Jersey Heritage/Société Jersiaise Collection (SJA/208)

Baron de Rullecourt (1744 - 1781)

Philippe Charles Felix Macquart was born in Flanders in what was then the Austrian Netherlands. He was an adventurer who may have simply taken the title of Baron rather than having it conferred or inherited. He reputedly abducted his wife, Marie Félicité, the illegitimate daughter of the Marquis d'Argenso, from a convent.

As befitted a gentleman from his background, he took up a career in the military and joined the Compagnie Flamande des Gardes du Corps in 1761. By 1767 he was a captain in the regiment of Nassau-Luxembourg and in 1769 he joined the French service. In 1774 he was a major in the cavalry and then he joined the Polish army as a colonel in the Massalski Regiment. He appears to have left Poland under a bit of a cloud and accusations of theft.

Sensing opportunity coming out of Britain's American Wars, he returned to France and in 1779 he sailed with the Prince of Nassau as second in command in the doomed attempt to capture Jersey. On his return he rejoined the French army as lieutenant colonel des volontaires de Luxembourg au service de France. A contemporary view of de Rullecourt comes from Dumouriez who describes him as *a roué in every sense of the word, head over ears in debt, who pays his creditors with sword thrusts and then puts himself at the head of those light-fingered gentry, the Luxembourg Volunteers, who pillaged Normandy from end to end as they marched along.*

St Helier from the Richmond Map surveyed within 10 years of the Battle of Jersey.

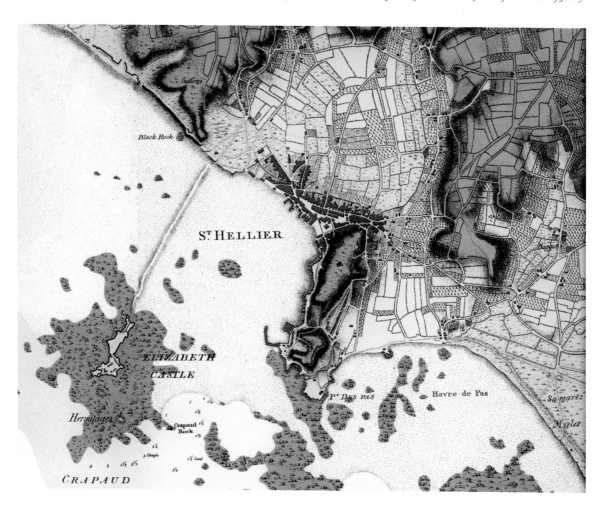

The view of St Helier from Mont Patibulaire (Gallows Hill) by George Heriot (1759 - 1839).

Jersey Heritage/Société Jersiaise Collection

The view of St Helier from the north by George Heriot (1759 - 1839).
Jersey Heritage/Société Jersiaise Collection

The view towards St Helier from Samares with Mont de la Ville in the middle distance by George Heriot (1759 - 1839).
Jersey Heritage/Société Jersiaise Collection

The timing of the Battle

Proceeding carefully in the dark and trying to keep his vessels close together, the French flotilla was about two miles offshore at about 8.00pm. By 10.00pm the tide had turned and the current began to push southwards causing them problems. By half tide at 11.00pm, the French fleet was off Point de la Rocque and the narrow channel leading into the rocky southeastern corner of Jersey. On the northern side of the channel is the Violet Bank - over two miles of gravel, shingle and sand interspersed with numerous ledges of sharp pointed rocks and, more importantly for de Rullecourt, covered by at least a foot of water with a three knot tidal current running over it.

The *Renard* with about 250 men on board ran aground and was seriously damaged. *L'Oiseau* carrying another 250 men, as well as the expedition's cannon and shot was swept away, missed the entrance to the channel and was forced to return to Chaussey. Monsieur d'Herville, a Major in the Legion of Luxembourg managed to join up with de Rullecourt in a small boat. He noted *the tide had been falling for about four hours, one of the obstacles the rear guard had to contend with was an insurmountable difficulty that the Banc de Violet was surrounded by jagged rocks*[10].

These two mishaps cost de Rullecourt about 500 fighting men as well as his artillery.

Because the approach to La Rocque is so narrow and difficult, progress was slow. The falling tide and poor visibility meant that some vessels were unable to complete their approach and so had to turn back for safer and deeper waters. *La Prudente* of Granville commanded by Pierre Bouret dit Le Rivière carrying more cannon and gunners missed the entrance and

so beat off the coast of Jersey until 11.00am on the morning of the 6th. *The London Gazette* for 13 January reported that the French force lost one privateer, four transport vessels were wrecked and over 200 men drowned.

The advance troops managed to surprise the guard at La Rocque guardhouse, take over the battery with its four nine-pounder cannon and secure a beachhead. The rest of the French troops began landing at about 2.00am. Although high water was at 2.35am it was a neap tide and so was only 26' 7" (8.09m) which meant the troops still had a fair way to travel before they were on dry land.

When all the troops were mustered on land, de Rullecourt found that instead of his 1,500 men and cannon, he was left with an invasion force of about 600 infantrymen.

Nevertheless, he decided to press on regardless and so left a rearguard of about 100 men and, reminding his men that the password was *Vive Le Roi et Luxembourg*, set off to march just over four and a half miles with the intention of reaching St Helier before daybreak.

Obviously de Rullecourt wanted to move his men as quickly as possible through the countryside yet at the same time, conscious of how much noise a column of 500 armed infantrymen make, he wanted to avoid built-up areas as much as possible. The most likely route to St Helier was along the coast as far as Rue de Jambart and then they would have struck inland through Rue de Prince and Rue de la Hougette and then over to La Blinerie.

A small detachment would have been sent to St Clement's Church to cut the bell rope so as to prevent or delay the alarm being raised.

Once the column reached the outskirts of Town, in the area we now know as Georgetown, de Rullecourt split his force. He took his column along the high road towards La Colomberie and the other took the low road which led towards Le Dicq to take the Engineers' Barracks at La Collette.

They were spotted as they marched down La Colomberie just before 6.00am when Elizabeth Messervy put her head out of the window to see what all the noise was. A couple of hundred yards further on they encountered Pierre Arrivé who had just left his house close to the steps leading to La Rue de Vents (Snow Hill). He was immediately bayoneted and killed. By 6.00am the French had reached the Market Square and secured the Court House. The noise of the French troops was such that it could not be ignored and people began to come to their doors to see what was happening. Jean De Ste Croix was bayoneted and struck on the head by a sword but managed to escape to a neighbour's house where his wounds were treated. One of the sentries in the Piquet House near the Square in Church Street was killed but the other managed to escape and ran to the Hospital, which was being used as a barracks for the 78th Regiment, and raised the alarm.

Moyse Corbet directing the defence of the Island in 1779 on the heights above St Ouen's Bay by Philippe Jean (1755 - 1802).
Jersey Heritage/Société Jersiaise Collection (SJA/58)

Moyse Corbet (1728 - 1817)

Major Moyse Corbet was the Jersey-born Lieutenant Governor at the time of the Battle. Following the successful repulsing of an attempted invasion two years earlier in 1779 he was regarded as a hero, yet following the events of January 1781 he became perhaps the most hated man in the Island. Corbet had been one of the men, along with Philippe Falle and Charles William Le Geyt, behind the anti-Charles Lemprière movement and the 1769 Corn Riots which lead to Bentinck's Code of 1771. He had been a regular soldier who retired on half pay at the end of the Seven Years War in 1763. Following Bentinck's recall in 1771, Corbet was appointed Lieutenant Governor in his place.

Corbet was arrested on 25 January and court martialled on 1 May 1781 at the Horse Guards, Whitehall, London on the grounds that he did *contrary to his duty and the trust reposed in him, sign with the Commander of the French Troops articles of capitulation...*

The second column had just reached Parker's house at Le Dicq (now the White Horse Inn) when the first alarm guns were fired.

Clement Hemery, Captain in the St Helier Battalion of the Jersey Militia, who lived in a house overlooking the Market Square saw what was going on and so dressed in dark clothing and left his house by the back door to raise the alarm. He made his way down Halkett Street to the open country behind La Rue du Milieu (Queen Street) and skirting town he reached the Governor's House, which was at the corner of what was to become Grosvenor Street and La Motte Street, about the same time as Captain Edward Combs.

Corbet was appraised of the situation and immediately implemented what must have been already laid down plans. Captain Hemery was given a horse and sent off to Fort Conway, Grouville to warn Captain Campbell and the 83rd of the invasion. A second officer, possibly Combs, was dispatched to La Hougue, St Peter to warn the 95th via the Hospital at the edge of Town and to warn the 78th.

De Rullecourt's men had captured Captain Charlton, Commander of the Invalid Company, and Pierre Amiraux, the noted silversmith, and forced them to lead the way to Corbet's residence. Unaware that they had missed Corbet's messengers by a matter of minutes, the French surrounded the house and by 7.00am the Lieutenant Governor, still in his nightshirt, was captured. Dressing hurriedly, he was escorted to the Court House where he was met by de Rullecourt who demanded that Corbet sign articles of surrender.

It was about 8.00am and the streets were beginning to lighten as the sun rose.

While all this activity was taking place in the eastern part of Town, Captain Lumsdaine, the commanding

How the capture of Corbet was shown in the newspapers of the day - surprised in his bed.
Jersey Heritage/Société Jersiaise Collection (SJA/2294)

The Governor surprized in Bed.

officer of the 78th Regiment of Foot who was lodging in *one of the cross back streets*[11], was informed by his servant that the enemy was in Town. He was joined almost immediately by Lieutenant MacRae who was lodging in the house next door and the pair of them made a run for it to join their men who were lodged on the outskirts of Town in the Hospital Barracks. Once clear of the houses they climbed over garden walls and made it to the barracks where they found the regiment had already been appraised of the situation (possibly by Edward Combs) and were making preparations for battle.

Captain Lumsdaine dispatched a sergeant to Major Peirson and the 95th Regiment of Foot - acquainting him of his intention to withdraw from Town, along with a six-pounder and a howitzer, to take position on Mont Patibulaire, overlooking Town and Elizabeth Castle about half a mile to the west and to await him. This was obviously planned for it allowed the regiment to withdraw in force to a prearranged rendezvous position from which they could dominate Town while they received accurate intelligence. As the alarms were sounded around the Island, militiamen began to arrive. Some of the first were the St Lawrence Battalion under their commander Colonel George Benest who arrived just after 8.00am.

Meanwhile Captain Mulcaster of the Engineers, who had also been warned of the enemy's presence by

a servant, left his house near the Market Square on horseback to go to his company at La Collette via the shoreline but, realising the position, he made for Elizabeth Castle instead. In Captain Aylward's absence, he took command of the artillery, and at about 7.15am the alarm gun was fired to warn the men at St Aubin's Fort who repeated the signal, which was then echoed by several batteries around the Island until the message reached Mont Orgueil. The Reverend Le Couteur of St Martin noted that he was awakened by the noise of the alarm guns at 7.20am. Alerted by the guns, the Militia began to gather at their rendezvous points where they received orders from Peirson to move on Mont Patibulaire.

Just after 9.00am Captain Lumsdaine received a letter from Mulcaster requesting that some of the militia gunners be sent to help man the cannon. Men from the St Lawrence Battalion were sent straight over to strengthen the castle garrison.

In the west of the Island Peirson received messages of the French invasion from Edward Combs, and of Lumsdaine's intentions from a sergeant of the 78th. Hearing the alarm cannons being fired around the Island, he knew that the Militia would be mustering. Peirson led the 95th eastwards towards Town where he joined up with Captain Lumsdaine and his five companies of the 78th Highland Regiment on Mont Patibulaire at about 10.00am and, as the senior British officer, assumed command.

The regulars were joined a few minutes later by Colonel Pipon and the men of the South West Militia (5th) Regiment. Over the next hour the North Militia (2nd) Regiment and men from the St Saviour companies of the East Militia (3rd) Regiment arrived.

Since the events of 1781 Town has greatly expanded and the names of the streets have changed from essentially French descriptive names to English. At the time of the Battle the main streets in Town were :

La Grand Rue	Broad Street
Mont Patibulaire	Gallows Hill/West Hill
La Rue de Froid Vents	Regent Road
La Rue de Trois Pigeons	Hill Street
La Rue Trousse Cotillons	Church Street
La Rue de Derrière	King Street
La Rue du Milieu	Queen Street
Place Marché/Market Square	Royal Square

The street that retains its old name is La Colomberie.

Negotiations

To ensure the success of his occupation, de Rullecourt needed to neutralise Elizabeth Castle and get the garrison there to surrender. Initially the French sent a demand for the surrender of the castle which was refused. An initial attempt on the castle was repulsed by cannon fire, killing two men and wounding others forcing the French to retire to Town. It was at this point Mulcaster sent his request for assistance to Captain Lumsdaine. As well as the militiamen from St Lawrence, Captain Aylward of the Invalids arrived at the castle and Mulcaster relinquished command ...*being the eldest officer, I gave up the command.*[12] Unaware that the garrison had been reinforced, a second party of French officers went out to demand the surrender of the Castle and again this was refused. No further discussion could take place for by now it was 10.45am and the incoming tide was covering the causeway.

All the time this was going on, de Rullecourt, who had been down to the shoreline to look at Elizabeth Castle, cannot have failed to notice red-coated troops marching from the west and gathering on Mont Patibulaire.

On his return to the Court House, where he had set up his headquarters, de Rullecourt had barricades placed across La Rue de Trois Pigeons (Hill Street) leading up from the harbour, and as he had lost his own artillery, he had the three St Helier militia cannon taken from the Church and placed in the western entrances to the Square, which was where he expected any attack to come from.

Events in St Helier

From Mont Patibulaire Peirson saw that the French were still in the Market Square and had taken no steps to occupy Mont de la Ville which dominated St Helier from the south. He immediately detached Captain Thomas Frazer of the 78th to secure this vantage point. With Thomas Pipon as guide, Frazer led a battalion company of the 78th along with the light companies from both the 78th and the 95th supported by the light company of the North Militia Regiment. Their orders were to take position on the north escarpment from where they could shoot down into the Market Square. While they took a circuitous route along the shoreline to approach Mont de la Ville from the harbour side to avoid being seen by the French, Peirson, probably as a diversionary tactic, sent Ensign Byne of the 95th Regiment under a flag of truce to ascertain whether Corbet was prisoner of the French and, if he was, to demand his release.

When a little time had elapsed Peirson gave the order to march on Town. Leaving the North West Militia (1st) Regiment, who had just arrived as the reserve, Peirson led the first column which was made up of the grenadier company and remaining eight battalion companies of the 95th accompanied by Colonel Pipon and the South West Militia (5th) Regiment. At their head was the howitzer. The second column headed by Captain Lumsdaine was made up of the remaining three battalion companies of the 78th and the militiamen of the South Militia (2/4th) Regiment, elements of the South Militia (1/4th) Regiment and the St Saviour companies of the East Militia (3rd) Regiment. They had the six-pounder with them which was placed under the charge of Lieutenant Crozier of the Invalid artillery assisted by Sergeant Menzies of the Militia artillery.

The plan was straightforward in that both columns would approach Town from across the sands (now the Parade). At Cheapside where the French had set up a small outpost in the arch of the Prison which straddled the road leading into Town, they would divide. Captain Lumsdaine would force his way through the narrow arch into La Grande Rue (Broad Street) and then lead his column in a frontal assault while Peirson would lead his column up La Rue de Derrière (King Street) in a flanking attack by entering the Square from the northeast corner. While this was going on Frazer's men would be harassing the enemy from the heights of Mont de la Ville by firing down into the Square and then once the main attack out of La Grande Rue (Broad Street) began, Frazer was to lead the regulars down into Town leaving the militiamen to continue firing down into the French ranks.

As the British advanced they were met at the outskirts of Town by Corbet and a French officer under a flag of truce. Corbet again ordered Peirson to surrender and again he refused. Corbet and the accompanying French officer asked for time to relay the refusal to de Rullecourt to which Peirson granted them ten minutes before his advance continued, after which the action resumed and the British forces began their advance. Lumsdaine's men forced the arch and advanced up La Grande Rue (Broad Street) to meet the enemy while Peirson's column swung around into La Rue de Derrière (King Street). Peirson's route had the advantage of being hidden from the French in the Market Square by buildings but they were equally ignorant of what was happening to Lumsdaine and his men.

The French had taken the three militia cannon from the Town Church and placed them in the entrances to

One of the earliest representations of the Battle in the Market Square.
The GLORIOUS DEFEAT of the FRENCH INVADERS on the ISLAND of JERSEY Jany 6 1781 when the valiant Major Pierson was unfortunately Kill'd in the moment of Victory, *published by Thom Gram Colley and E Hedges, 24 April 1781.*
Jersey Heritage/Société Jersiaise Collection (SJA/2303)

the Square. The two placed by the Town Guard House were pointed straight down into La Grande Rue (Broad Street) in the direction of the advancing Scots. The inexperienced French gunners set them too high and when the first was fired at 40 metres the shot sailed harmlessly over the advancing troops. Seeing this, the men tending the second cannon panicked and fled, abandoning both cannon. Lumsdaine ordered his men to halt and the six-pounder, charged with either grape or case-shot, was fired several times, ripping great holes in the French ranks, before it was hauled to the right, allowing the 78th to follow up with volley fire before charging with fixed bayonets.

At the same time the fire from Frazer's men on Mont de la Ville was so intense that many of the French took shelter in the houses surrounding the Square.

Meanwhile Peirson at the head of his grenadier company led his men into the Square. Realising that his men were in danger of being caught in the Scots' line of fire he was motioning his men back when he was struck by a bullet. In the confusion of the fight it may have been a British musket which fired the fatal shot. His men dragged him back into the safety of Mrs Fiott's house (now Burton's) where he died.

The 95th had withdrawn about 50 metres back into La Rue de la Derrière (King Street) where it was said that one of their sergeants and Lt Philippe Durrell of the South West Militia (5th) Regiment rallied the men and led them back into the Square. However, on 22 February the States of Jersey recorded their thanks to Captain (now Major) James Corbet for taking command of the 95th Regiment following the death of Peirson and his role as chief mourner at Peirson's funeral would seem to back this situation.

Finding themselves attacked from all sides the French began to waver and, according to a letter written by Moyse Corbet the following day, the French officers withdrew into the Court House. De Rullecourt emerged from the Court House with the Lieutenant Governor at his side, possibly with the intention of surrendering, when he was struck by musket balls fired by the 78th Highlanders. Two balls passed through his thigh, a third went through his neck and a fourth shattered his jaw. Miraculously Corbet, despite having his hat shot away, survived unscathed. De Rullecourt was carried over to Dr Lerrier's House on the east side of the Square where he died six hours later.

By 12.30pm the fighting was over - it had lasted about 15 minutes.

With Peirson dead, Corbet resumed command of the British forces in the Island as the French prisoners were rounded up. The rank and file were held in the Town Church and the Officers were held in the Court House.

The Butcher's Bill

It was a sharp engagement in the Square and the British forces got away quite lightly losing only ten men killed - six regulars (including their commander) and four militiamen, with 29 regulars wounded and between 20 and 26 militiamen wounded. A best guess would be that the French lost 58 killed (including their commander) in the Square, about 56 wounded and about 290 men taken prisoner.

At the engagement at Platte Rocque the regulars lost seven men and seven men wounded and the militia suffered between one and three men wounded while the French lost 20 killed and 30 taken prisoner of whom 18 were wounded.

78th Regiment

light company:	1 rank & file killed
	3 rank & file wounded
battalion company:	2 rank & file killed
	12 rank & file wounded

83rd Regiment

| grenadier company: | 7 rank & file killed[13] |
| | 7 rank & file wounded |

95th Regiment

| | 1 officer & 2 rank & file killed |
| | 1 sergeant & rank & file wounded |

Total: 1 officer, 11 rank & file killed, 1 sergeant & 35 rank & file wounded (plus Captain Charlton of the Invalids wounded whilst being taken prisoner)

Militia

NW Regiment	1 rank & file wounded
East Regiment	2 lieutenants[14], 1 ensign[15],
	6 rank & file wounded
St Lawrence Battalion	2 rank & file killed[16]
	6 rank & file wounded
St Helier Battalion	2 rank & file killed
	10 rank & file wounded
SW Regiment	3 rank & file wounded

Total: 4 rank & file killed, 3 officers & 26 rank & file wounded

Civilians

1 killed, wounded unknown

French casualties

78 killed, 74 wounded and 417 taken prisoner

Events at La Rocque

By the time all the troops had landed and mustered at La Rocque and been organised into their relevant sections, it must have been well after four in the morning. Once de Rullecourt had moved off with his men to march towards St Helier the soldiers left behind as a rearguard do not appear to have done much.

At about 7.20 am the Reverend Francis Le Couteur, rector of St Martin, was awakened by the noise of the alarm guns being fired around the Island. Dressing quickly he received reports that there were a number of vessels lying at anchor amongst the rocks *of St Clements*[17]. He sent out one of his servants to get better information. On his return he reported that there were about 12-14 small cutters and brigs close to the shore. This information was further supplemented by the arrival of Jean Laugée, a gunsmith, who had been wounded as he escaped Town. He told Le Couteur that French forces were in Town and that both Corbet and his wife had been taken captive.

Alerted by the alarm guns the men of the North Militia (2nd) Regiment began to assemble at their rendezvous

Fort Conway by an artist of the English School c.1850.
Jersey Heritage/Société Jersiaise Collection (SJA/759)

points and the militia cannon were removed from the Church. Following their prearranged plan they would head south towards Mont Patibulaire. The Reverend Le Couteur, the personification of the Church Militant, however, decided to take his two personal cannon and a small detachment of gunners down to Fort Conway.

The alarms that woke Le Couteur also alerted Captain Campbell of the 83rd Regiment who was stationed in Fort Conway (Fort Henry) on Grouville Common. In the morning half light the French shipping off La Rocque must have become visible and so while he awaited further intelligence, he drew up his five companies outside the fort where they were joined by detachments of the East Militia (3rd) Regiment.

Unaware of the situation in Town, Campbell dispatched Lieutenant Niven to Corbet for instructions. Unfortunately, Niven was captured by the French forces as soon as he arrived at Corbet's house. The fact that they had not met on the way would seem to indicate that Captain Hemery had taken a slightly longer route, possibly via La Hougue Bie, in order to avoid any French.

Shortly after Hemery's appearance the Reverend Francis Le Couteur arrived at Fort Conway with his cannon eager to engage the enemy. Campbell, an experienced officer, resisted all of Le Couteur's attempts at getting him to attack straight away. At about 9.00am he had one of his men mounted on horseback and sent forward to reconnoitre the position. The scout reported seeing prisoners being taken into the La Rocque battery by French soldiers. This may have been Hemery[18] who claims to have been captured as he returned to St Helier having decided to take a closer look at the French disposition. (Hemery later escaped under the pretence of negotiating with

the militia, although the question must be asked, would a gentleman have given his parole and then broken it? Certainly Corbet and Captain Charlton did not). About the same time four militiamen arrived at Fort Conway leading about two dozen French prisoners who they had gathered up from the beach, who were probably some of those lost from the *Renard* or *L'Oiseau*.

The French rearguard finally decided upon a course of action and so sent a demand, written in French, to Campbell requiring the surrender of the 83rd. Campbell's response was to advance his men, along with militia and Le Couteur's cannon towards La Rocque.

The French commander of the rearguard recognised that he was outnumbered and so sent a sergeant forward to parley with the advancing British troops. At the same time his men belatedly started to turn the nine-pounders of the battery towards the advancing British troops. Seeing this activity in the battery Campbell broke off the parley, placed his four line companies behind a wall in front of the enemy and ordered Lieutenant Robertson with about 40 of the grenadiers and ten militiamen led by Lieutenant Helier Godfray to fix bayonets and attack the French flank while he led the other half company of grenadiers towards the other flank. At a distance of about eight metres Robertson ordered the French to surrender, the French rear rank opened fire killing one grenadier and immediately the grenadiers returned a volley and then charged with bayonets. The British rush forward killed 20 men and took more than 30 prisoners of whom 18 were wounded all for the loss of five more men and eight wounded (one of whom subsequently died of his wounds).

Captain William Campbell

Commander of the 83rd Regiment in the absence from the Island of his senior officers. Campbell was described in *The Edinburgh Evening Courant* of 20 January 1781 as so *able an officer... who had before remarkably distinguished himself.* Some have seen his actions at La Rocque as indecision borne out of fear of losing his commission for disobeying a superior officer, however a letter from an anonymous officer of the 83rd published in *The Edinburgh Evening Courant* of the 22 January 1781 puts the reluctance to act down to his natural caution to act without reliable information on the numbers of French troops, their disposition and the location of their landing places.

With the battery secure and the French rearguard destroyed, Campbell withdrew his men to Fort Conway leaving the militia and the Reverend Le Couteur to hold the position. Le Couteur turned his cannon and those of the battery on the escaping French soldiers hiding amongst the rocks and any small boat dispatched by the anchored French ships to take them off.

Campbell was back at Fort Conway when Lieutenant Snow of the St Helier Militia arrived at Fort Conway carrying orders from Corbet demanding the 83rd surrender. Campbell's dilemma was swiftly resolved when another militiaman, Lieutenant Thomas Anley, arrived bearing a message from Major Peirson of the 95th saying, *make haste to come to our assistance, we are going to engage.*

By the time the 83rd reached St Helier, the French had been defeated and the Town was once more back under British control. Over the next few days the remaining French troops who had escaped into the Island were rounded up and the Island remained on alert.

The aftermath

On 7 January HMS *Minerva* was ordered to carry the French prisoners to England along with a guard of one captain, two subalterns, three sergeants, three corporals, two drummers and 44 privates drawn from various of the Island's militia regiments in order to prevent any petty jealousies breaking out. The bulk of the prisoners were landed in Plymouth on Tuesday 9 January.[19]

Peirson was buried in St Helier Church with full military honours on Wednesday 10 January. His coffin was accompanied by the eldest officer in the garrison and Captain James Corbet of the 95th was named as Chief Mourner. The procession was headed by his regiment and the Island Clergy and was followed by Island administration - the Lieutenant Governor and Lieutenant Bailiff, the Jurats and the Gentlemen of the Island.

The fall out began almost immediately. *The London Gazette* on 9 January commented that an officer's duty and honour *should equally forbid them to absent themselves... in time of war... It was therefore unpardonable in General Conway to be absent from his Government of Jersey, at the season of the year when his presence was most necessary.* Action had to be taken and so on 17 January 1781 Corbet was forced to stand down as Lieutenant Governor and, ironically, was replaced temporarily by Colonel John Reid of the 95th Regiment who had returned to the Island following the news of the Battle.

Following the fighting a number of officers received promotions. In the 95th Regiment Captain James Corbet replaced Peirson as Major, Lieutenant Gilbert Waugh was made up to Captain to replace Corbet, Ensign Charles Byne was made up to Lieutenant and John Samuel Locke, gentleman volunteer,[20] was made Ensign. In the 83rd Regiment where no officer died there must have been a vacancy because Ensign David Fleming replaced John French as Lieutenant, and Philippe Nicole who had been serving as a gentleman volunteer was made Ensign.

The strategic importance of what had been attempted did not escape the newspapers either. On 13 January, *The Oxford Journal* commented that *the capture of the Isle of Jersey was planned as a Diversion and intended to prevent the country from sending her Navy to the relief of Gibraltar, and upon other services.*

Corbet was arrested on 25 January and recalled to England where on 1 May 1781 he was court martialled at the Horse Guards, Whitehall, London on the grounds that he *did contrary to his duty and the trust reposed in him, sign with the Commander of the French Troops articles of capitulation...* He was tried by three generals, four colonels and eight lieutenant colonels. The trial lasted five days.

The main witnesses were:

Day One: Prosecution
    Frederick De La Taste - civilian
    Joshua Le Gros - civilian
    John Lauger (Laugée) - civilian, gunsmith
    Peter Amiraux - civilian, silversmith
    Captain Charlton - Invalid Artillery
    Colonel Durell - Jersey Militia

Day Two: Prosecution
    Mrs Penny - St Helier innkeeper
    Captain Mulcaster - Royal Engineers

Captain Lumsdaine - 78th Regiment
Lieutenant Niven - 83rd Regiment

Day Three: Prosecution
    Reverend Francis Le Couteur - Rector of St Martin
    Lieutenant Byne - 95th Regiment
    Lieutenant Harrison - 95th Regiment
    Francis Kirkby

Day Four: Defence
    Major Corbet - Lieutenant Governor and defendant
    Mr Combe
    Mr Combe jnr - Militia man
    Captain Hemery - St Helier Militia
    Captain Mulcaster - Royal Engineers
    Captain Messervy - Militia
    Lieutenant Anley - St Helier Militia

Day Five: Defence
    Lieutenant Anley - St Helier Militia
    Mr Bertram - Merchant
    Mathieu De la Cloche - Constable of St Helier
    Captain Patriarche - Militia
    Lord Robert Bertie - character witness

The court martial found Corbet guilty and the verdict was that he should be replaced as Lieutenant Governor. However, he was granted a pension of £250 per year, which was the equivalent of the full pay of a serving major in the British army. Corbet never returned to the Island and lived in seclusion for the rest of his life. He died in France in 1817 at the age of 89. At the trial nothing was said about all three commanding officers and their subordinates of the garrison regiments in the Island having been on leave at the same time at a time when the enemy was less than a day's sail away; indeed Colonel John Reid of the 95th Regiment had been one of them.

Perhaps to paraphrase Voltaire, Corbet had been sacrificed to encourage others.

Geometric composition

Behind the chaos of battle the artist has created a complex geometric structure. A triangle is formed by the fallen sergeant, fleeing women and regimental flag. This encourages the viewer's eye to wander around the picture, taking in the whole scene. The focus of the picture is in the centre of the triangle. As a viewer your eye is led up the arm of the fallen sergeant towards the right along the dark hats of the officers in the central group and then turning left with the face of the officer in profile, then down the white leg of Peirson to his face and then along his arm to the pool of blood on the floor.

The setting

Copley probably never travelled to Jersey to make sketches of the Battle location. He may have sent his half-brother, Henry Pelham to make drawings for him, or asked Islanders living in London for their first-hand knowledge of the battlefield.

The Highlanders

The 78th Highlanders fought in the Battle but Copley has demoted them from active participants to bit-part players. He includes them in the background firing from the hill above, in the main body of the picture as two figures in the background firing on the French and as a dead soldier lying on the battlefield alongside his bonnet. Copley surmised that an obvious presence of the Scottish would not be popular with his English audience who considered the Battle an English victory.

e confusion of battle

ong diagonal lines and high contrast
ght and dark intensify the drama and
fusion of battle.

Loyalty to the monarchy

The statue of George II is revealed through the smoke of battle, giving the location as what is now Royal Square. The statue of the monarch suggests loyalty to the Crown and reinforces the location as being a British territory.

Baron de Rullecourt lies in the arms of his comrades at the door of the Court House. The Royal Arms is patriotically revealed through a gap in the smoke. The French leader lies dead or dying at the steps of a building which represents British justice and rule, and symbolically at the feet of a British monarch.

Revenge

Amidst the noise and chaos of battle, a servant, known as Pompey, avenges Peirson's death. Behind Pompey, a captain directs his aim. A puff of smoke indicates that the trigger has just been released and in the time it takes your eye to cross the canvas, the musket ball has found its target. The leader of the French forces, Baron de Rullecourt, lies dying in the arms of his comrades.

Civilians

This small group of fleeing figures are the only civilians in the battle scene. Their expressions of fear and horror are in stark contrast to the stoic expressions of many of the military figures. They run forward, almost out of the picture. The young boy looks out of the picture directly at us, making us see the horror of battle though his eyes. Copley used his own son, John Singleton Copley junior as the model for this figure and his wife and children's nurse as the model for the women.

The Death of Major Peirson, *1783 by John Singleton Copley.*
© *Tate, London 2011 (N00733)*

The Death of Major Peirson -
the theatre of war by Louise Downie

The Death of Major Peirson 1782 - 84 by John Singleton Copley (1738 - 1815) is an enduring image of heroism and sacrifice. An epic history painting, which combines fact and fiction, the painting has, for many Jersey people, become part of the Island's psyche. Continual reproduction and re-use of the image means that 'The Battle of Jersey' as it is colloquially known is held in Jersey's collective memory as an iconic representation of the Island's contentious past. That this phenomenon still prevails more than 200 years after the painting's creation stands testament to its success as a history painting.

The mythology of *The Death of Major Peirson* purports that at one stage in its history, a print of the painting would have hung in every Jersey household. In general, its viewers have been less interested in the 'how' or 'why' of its existence and more concerned with its depiction of the ultimate noble sacrifice amidst the heat of battle, the patriotism this represents and the feelings of nationhood and pride it generates. The Battle of Jersey itself was a relatively short invasion, defence and victory, but one which had significant and momentous consequences for the Island's future. It led to an extensive programme of building defensive structures throughout the Island, including the construction of a ring of towers around the coast. But, perhaps more significant than the physical reminders of the Battle's consequences are the long-term effects on the Island's status as a British frontier close to an often hostile French coast. The painting is a visual reminder of the Island's vulnerability and loyalty. The fact that the Battle itself lasted a matter of minutes is of little interest when confronted with an image of

bravery, stoicism, revenge and terror and of the British Nation's belligerence towards any threat to the status quo and willingness to fight to the death to maintain territories and loyalties. The painting has ensured that the Battle is remembered with pride and a sense of patriotic nationhood and that Major Peirson remains a much-loved hero.

Can we, and should we, look to the painting as an accurate description of the events of that fateful day? How did Copley go about creating an image which encapsulated the story of the events of 6 January 1781 into one single moment? Why did he decide to include some events and people and exclude others? How does Copley make us, the audience, feel part of the picture and empathetic towards those taking part in the Battle? How did Copley, much like a theatrical impresario or film director, direct the action of the painting and affect our responses to it? How did he make the Battle of Jersey such a memorable event? How does *The Death of Major Peirson* compare to more recent war paintings and do they serve the same purpose and have the same effect?

News of the Battle of Jersey reaches London

Copley was an American artist who settled himself and his family in London, the 'in' place for an English-speaking ambitious artist keen to create and publicise his art and to receive lucrative portrait commissions.

Like other members of London society, Copley would no doubt have heard news of the Battle and Peirson's bravery through word-of-mouth and newspaper reports. In contrast to today's instant and up to the minute news reporting, news carried via mail ships from an isolated outpost would have taken a while to arrive. The first sketchy reports of the invasion and Battle appeared in the London and regional newspapers a few days after the event. Relatively little was known about Jersey amongst the general populace in Britain and some newspapers even felt the need to give their readers some information on the Island: *Jersey is an Island in the English Channel, situated 15 miles west of the coast of Normandy, in France, and 80 miles south of Portland, in Dorsetshire, subject to Great Britain; it is about 30 miles in circumference, difficult to access, on account of the rocks, sands and forts, erected for its defence; it contains twelve parishes, the chief town is St.Hillary (sic), in the south of the Island, there is more fruit than corn in the Island, and it is well watered with rivulets. It lies extremely well for trade in times of peace, and to annoy the French with their privateers in time of war. They have a good woollen manufactory of stockings, caps &C. They are descended from French ancestors, and are still governed by Norman laws.*[21] Readers were obviously keen for news of the Battle as an Edinburgh editor even apologised for not being able to bring more up-to-date reports, blaming adverse winds preventing mail boats from docking nearby.[22]

By mid-January full reports were readily available to a fascinated public. It is likely that Copley read some of these reports and it is worth recounting a selection in order to gain insight into the public's perception of the battle and in particular of Major Peirson's role, but also to give a linguistic flavour of the day. Major Peirson was singled out for praise, *The brave Major Peirson was killed in the moment of victory... Much praise is due to all*

the troops, regulars and Islanders, for their immediate exertions, courage and intrepidity; and with the much lamented Major Peirson, many others are mentioned as having greatly exerted themselves.[23] A letter from Jersey dated January 10 1781 printed in *The Edinburgh Evening Courant* on January 22 1781 used highly emotive language to describe the death of Major Peirson, *On our side, we suffered the irreparable loss of poor Major Peirson, who was shot through the heart just as VICTORY declared herself for him, to the regret of everybody; no other officer killed or wounded; very few privates killed or wounded.*

Major Peirson was interred this afternoon about three o'clock, in the parish church of St.Hilary (sic), in this Island with all the military funeral pomp possible; every regiment attended, with the Lieutenant Governor, the States of the Island, and all the militia officers, in short, no man could be more loved or respected, or lamented than he is. He died in the arms of Victory, aged 23.[24]

In contrast Lieutenant Governor Corbet, the senior commander on the Island was criticised for the confused nature of his reports, *The despatches (sic) (probably from being written in a moment of great perturbation of mind by the Lieutenant Governor, the day after the affair) are drawn up in so confused a stile (sic), that Government will not, as we learn, give the public any further account, till they receive a more intelligible and collected state of particulars.*[25]

Peirson's actions throughout the day were fully recounted in the newspapers, which reported that upon receiving and refusing to accept Corbet's order to capitulate, Peirson immediately took control, gathering forces and information on French troop numbers. *Such was the zeal and activity of the late Major Peirson, in service of his country that the artillery men being absent when the French appeared in St.Hilier (sic),*

The FRENCH Attack on the Island of JERSEY or the Monsieurs Mistaken *by E Hedges published in November 1781.*
Library of Congress, PC 3 - 1781

The FRENCH Attack on the Island of JERSEY or the Monsieurs Mistaken

that he helped to harness the horses, and with his own hands put them in carriages, that no time might be lost in moving the cannon.[26] Captains Aylward and Mulcaster were similarly combative at Elizabeth Castle. Mulcaster shot at French forces when they neared the castle, injuring a French officer. He reportedly told an envoy, Mr D'Auvergne, that he *would not surrender the castle, or the British flag, so long as he had a man to defend it.*[27] Captain Aylward sent a belligerent letter to Corbet from Elizabeth Castle, *Sir, you being surprised and a prisoner, the command of his Majesty's troops on the Island devolves on Major Peirson, who we know is not surprised, or a prisoner, neither is this castle under my command. You know our situation and strength; and when we reflect*

that the British flag has received honour from the defence of this garrison in former times, we will not suffer its lustre to be diminished, and are therefore determined to hold out till the last.
I have the honour to be sir, your most obedient servant,
P AYLWARD.[28]

Further details of the day's events were reported in the accounts of Corbet's court martial held in May 1781, when he was charged with *having suffered the Island, under his command, to be surprised by the French, and for having signed articles of capitulation whilst he was a prisoner.*[29] Peirson's heroic actions were once again publicly lauded, *Major Peirson then told him (Corbet), he would rather die than give up the Island, and sent him back to tell the French general that he would attack in ten minutes* stated one witness.[30]

To the public mind Peirson, and to a lesser extent his fellow officers, fulfilled the role of a hero, the French the villains and Corbet the coward. Accounts of the heroic Battle and ignominious defeat of French forces appealed to the nation's pride and to anti-French feeling of the time, a result of centuries of war and discord. The situation at this time was particularly tense because in 1778 when the French became allies of the Americans in their fight against Britain, Jersey, being loyal to Britain was effectively just 15 miles from a hostile coast. In 1781, the Americans' fight for independence seemed increasingly likely to succeed. Reports of the Battle of Jersey often appeared in newspapers alongside news of developments in the American War of Independence. The decisive Battle of Yorktown was fought during the summer of 1781, a critical victory for the combined American and French forces led by General Washington (1732 - 99) and the Comte de Rochambeau (1725 - 1807). This was the last major land battle of the American Revolutionary War in North America, and was a demoralising defeat for the British Army. The French support for the American bid for independence made them a target for British nationalistic propaganda, so the failure of their attempted invasion of Jersey provided an opportunity to ridicule the French army. A cartoon entitled *The FRENCH Attack on the Island of JERSEY or the Monsieurs Mistaken* published by E Hedges showed miserable French soldiers being driven into the sea by smiling British soldiers. It was printed in November 1781, some months after the Battle of Jersey but more significantly after the British military defeat by the American and French combined forces at the Battle of Yorktown.

Contemporary history painting

At the end of the eighteenth century it was still unusual for artists to paint a contemporary historical event. Copley was breaking new ground by painting what was happening at the time rather than what had happened in the ancient past. Fellow American artist Benjamin West was criticised for using contemporary dress in his painting *The Death of General Wolfe*, 1770 and it was suggested that he clothe the figures in classical robes. Traditional history painting, usually of Biblical or literary themes, offered an idealised, often heroic world. Courage, glory and compassion had usually been portrayed in art by painting heroes from this distant, classical past. History painting was considered of the highest status in the hierarchy of artistic subjects particularly by the first president of the Royal Academy, Joshua Reynolds. Indeed the Royal Academy was originally founded in an effort to encourage and support history painting because it depicted profound human emotions, the study of which, it was believed, would ennoble the spectator and encourage similar feelings of fortitude and fearlessness. No other genre of art, be it portrait, landscape or still life was considered its equal. Copley and West persisted in painting modern events, eventually winning through with their combination of historical accuracy on detail and a dramatised version of the event. Copley was an experienced history painter, previous subjects having included *The Ascension*, 1775, *The Nativity*, 1776 - 77 and *Samuel Relating to Eli the Judgements of God Upon Eli's House*, 1780. West and Copley were the first artists to paint contemporary historical subjects. Copley's most recent work was *The Death of the Earl of Chatham*, 1779 - 81, a portrayal of the death of William Pitt, First Earl of Chatham, who collapsed in the House of Lords whilst replying to the Duke of Richmond's speech in favour of American independence. Copley and West's approach was innovative because by painting modern day events they drew attention to the heroism of the present day, and made it seem an equal to that of the past whilst borrowing the grandeur and gravitas of classical history painting.

One of the most important things that Copley had learnt from *The Death of the Earl of Chatham* and the earlier work *Watson and the Shark*, 1778 was that successful contemporary history painting combined factual accuracy with an often idealised, sanitised version of events. The sequence or location of events and people could be altered to create a more dramatic or emotional painting but the public would only

accept this if it were combined with a high level of precision on the details of clothing, portraits and setting. Copley surmised from the public reception of both his and Benjamin West's history paintings, that the public had an appetite for subjects with a strong nationalistic narrative conveyed in a powerful, visually exciting and uncompromising way, making the subject of their painting into a memorable event. It was not simply Copley's aim to create a visual record. He was not interested in merely reporting the facts. Like his predecessors who had painted history pictures, he felt it was his responsibility as an artist to elevate that reality to a level beyond pure reportage and thereby portray and praise values such as selfless heroism and sacrifice.

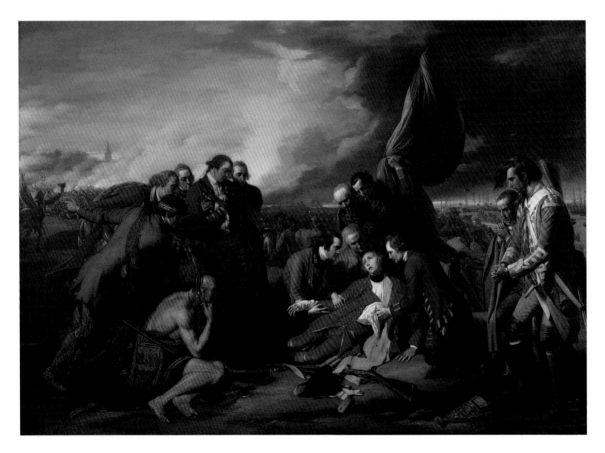

The Death of General Wolfe, *1770 by Benjamin West.*
The National Gallery of Canada, Ottawa

The commission

Major Peirson's heroic sacrifice, the reported valiant efforts of his fellow officers and soldiers and the defeat of the French appealed to Copley as a subject which would engage the nation's pride and reverence, a sense of loyalty with which Copley could empathise. Copley was an American artist, born in Boston, Massachusetts. His loyalty to the British Crown was one of the reasons he left Boston in 1774, when the political situation seemed increasingly turbulent. Painting such an event would enhance his reputation as a history painter, reaffirm his political loyalties and hopefully be well received by the public and critics. Copley established himself in London as a successful portrait and history painter. History painting was an expensive business and was highly unlikely to pay for itself. So that he did not bear the entire financial burden of creating such an epic painting himself, Copley formed a partnership with entrepreneur John Boydell, who had an established and successful printmaking and selling business. Copley accepted a commission from Boydell and the payment of £800, although he did not sign the contract with Boydell until May 1783. Perhaps he was hoping to receive a commission instead from the States of Jersey, who in April 1781 decided to commission a memorial to Peirson. However this commission was awarded to sculptor John Bacon, whose memorial to Peirson still stands in the Town Church of St Helier.

History paintings like *The Death of Major Peirson* while popular with the public were difficult to sell, as they were usually large and expensive. Boydell's plan was to create a print of the painting, the sale of which would finance the commission, making the image more widely distributable and providing an affordable and practical copy for the general public. The painting would be exhibited in a one-painting show with a one-shilling entrance fee, thereby generating further income. At this exhibition, visitors were encouraged to subscribe to buying a copy of the print. Creating original prints was expensive and Boydell gambled that the costs would be recovered and a profit made. His gambles usually paid off and he became the most successful printmaker in London. The print of *The Death of Major Peirson* was hugely popular and Boydell more than made his money back. His position as a civic-minded businessman culminated in being made the Lord Mayor of London in 1790. Copley was

Print of the monument in the interior of St Helier Church by P J Ouless. The memorial to Major Peirson by John Bacon.
Jersey Heritage/Société Jersiaise Collection (SJA/1797)

criticised by his artistic peers for the commercialism of the exhibition and print approach, many of whom regarded this practice as vulgar and un-gentlemanly. Leading members of the Royal Academy were also irked by the possibility that Copley's exhibition could poach visitors from their summer exhibition. Copley and Boydell were innovative in their marketing of the painting, opening up a new realm of self-funding art patronage which was not only beneficial to the artist and print-seller, but also to the public who were able to view the painting in a setting other than the Royal Academy and were able to buy a print of the painting, thereby keeping it alive in their visual memory.

Preparatory work

There is no evidence that Copley travelled to Jersey to sketch the battlefield location, and it seems most likely that he sent his half-brother Henry Pelham to perform this task. Like his father, Copley's stepfather, Henry Pelham was an engraver. He followed Copley to London in 1776 and Copley often sent him to sketch sites for him.[31] Another possible source of information for Copley was other London-based artists who had visited or lived in Jersey. Dominic Serres (1719 - 93), a founder member of the Royal Academy, visited Jersey in 1764 and painted one of the earliest oil paintings of the Island, *Elizabeth Castle, Jersey*. Jersey-born artist Philippe Jean (1755 - 1802) lived in London in the 1780s, making frequent return visits to his native Island.[32] Indeed Serres and Jean knew each other as Jean painted Serres' portrait in 1788. Jean also knew one of the main protagonists in the events of 6 January 1781, having painted Lieutenant Governor Major Moyse Corbet manning the stockades, a depiction of Corbet's successful repelling of an earlier French attack in 1779 (see page 24). This portrait is not up to Jean's

usual standards and may have been partly painted by someone else. Copley had a number of sources of information on the visual appearance of the location of the Battle and could have used a combination of some or all of these available sources.

Copley would no doubt have seen the earliest visual depiction of events, a print by Colley and Hedges published in London on 24 April 1781 entitled *The GLORIOUS DEFEAT of the FRENCH INVADERS on the ISLAND of JERSEY Jany 6 1781 when the valiant Major Pierson (sic) was unfortunately kill'd in the moment of victory* (see page 28). The print depicts two groups of soldiers separated by a line of guns and billowing smoke. The group on the right are the retreating French being advanced upon by the British to the left. The 78th Highlanders, identified by their kilts and tam-o-shanters, are clearly active in the battle. The ground is littered with dead bodies and a fallen drum. Accounts of the battle reported that Peirson was shot as he rounded a corner into the Market Square, as is shown on the far left of this print. A Highlander moves towards the falling figure. This print is a piece of reportage rather than an epic history painting, a piece of visual news reporting which lacks the visual ferocity of Copley's battle scene. Copley had a different agenda, he wanted to create a painting which was more than pure reportage, he aimed to create an image which would be memorable, heroic and empathetic. He was fully aware of the propaganda value of a British victory to a hugely patriotic late eighteenth century audience. He wished to capture the spirit of nationalistic fervour present in English society and sensed the national appeal of this albeit modest military victory. Copley also aspired to confirming his position as one of the leading artists in London society. He needed to create a painting which appealed to the public and which they would like to keep a small piece of in the form of a print.

Study for The Death of Major Peirson, *1782 - 84 by John Singleton Copley.*
Photograph © 2012 Museum of Fine Arts, Boston (1939.267a)

Study for the central group of The Death of Major Peirson, *1782 - 84 by John Singleton Copley.*
Photograph © 2012 Museum of Fine Arts, Boston (1939.268a)

Study for the central group of The Death of Major Peirson, *c.1783 by John Singleton Copley.*
© Tate, London 2011, London (N04984)

In order to create an accurate and dramatic history painting Copley began collecting information on the Battle, interviewing officers and making sketches of them and their uniforms. Preparatory sketches of the painting demonstrate his experimentation with poses and settings and reveal much about his working methods. They are verification of Copley's careful consideration of each and every detail that went into his painting. His skill as an artist is to transform his calculated decisions on every element into a painting that appears to be an uncomplicated and seamless portrayal of events. The sketches give us an idea of how Copley worked. Although it is not known in what order they were made, it is possible to make an educated guess.[33]

The buildings in Copley's scene-setting sketches and the horizontal block of figures resemble Colley and Hedges' print (top left and centre left). For Colley and Hedges the death of Major Peirson was an ancillary incident to the main theme of their news story which was the defeat of the French. In this sketch (top left), Copley has already relocated Major Peirson from the innocuous corner of the picture to the centre of the scene, establishing this incident as the focal point of the painting. It is apparent from the newspaper reports of the Battle that Major Peirson was the undisputed hero of the event. His death at the age of just 23 was presented as both heroic and tragic. Copley speculated that it was his death which most captured the public's imagination and should therefore be the main focus of his painting. In this sketch (middle left), Copley experiments with the positioning and gestures of some of the main characters - the fleeing group to the right, the marksman aiming his gun and the back view of an officer with his sword raised leading his troops into action. In another sketch (middle right), Copley left out some of the background figures and enlarged the central grouping. He moved the marksman to the right of the central grouping, and this time has another figure standing behind the marksman, directing his aim. Perhaps, in his search for accuracy, Copley had discovered that it was the practice in the British army for an officer to stand behind a marksman to point out their target.[34] In a number of sketches, Copley experimented with the grouping of the central figures and tested out a variety of poses for Peirson's dead body. In one sketch (see page 46 bottom left) Peirson is supported by a figure in a tam-o-shanter and kilt and is flanked by a monk presumably giving the last rites to the dying Peirson. Copley settled on the pose closest to that of the deposition, that is Christ being taken down from the cross, thereby comparing Peirson's death with Christ's martyrdom. Peirson dies in the arms of his comrades, delivering the noblest sacrifice. Captain Clement Hemery, wearing clerical black stands behind Peirson and his comrades, his hand raised in alarm, but also in a pose similar to that of the benediction, furthering the Biblical associations of Peirson's death. Copley obviously had this association in mind when he sketched a monk standing alongside Peirson, but chose to depict a more subtle religious connection in the final painting. Hemery was indeed wearing black rather than the red Militia uniform he should have been wearing because, having spotted the French as they approached the Market Square, he sneaked out of his back door to go and raise the alarm and did not want to wear an obviously military uniform. Hemery was then sent by Corbet to warn Captain Campbell of the 83rd Regiment in Grouville of the invasion. He might have had time to return to the Market Square if he had managed to acquire a horse somewhere along the way. Copley experimented with the placing of other groups, gradually adding shading, details, clothing and expressions. He used his wife, children and their nurse as the models for the group of fleeing women and children on the right.

Study for The Death of Major Peirson, *1782 - 84 by John Singleton Copley.*
Photograph © 2012 Museum of Fine Arts, Boston (39.268b)

Study for the central group of The Death of Major Peirson, *1782 - 83 by John Singleton Copley.*
The Samuel Courtauld Trust, The Courtauld Gallery, London (D.1952.RW.553)

Study for the central group of The Death of Major Peirson, *1782 - 84 by John Singleton Copley.*
Photograph © 2012 Museum of Fine Arts, Boston (39.269)

Study for The Death of Major Peirson, *1782 - 83 by John Singleton Copley.*
The Samuel Courtauld Trust, The Courtauld Gallery, London (D.1952.RW.295)

Study for the fleeing women and child in The Death of Major Peirson, *1782 - 83 by John Singleton Copley.*
Photograph © 2012 Museum of Fine Arts, Boston (39.267b)

Study for the The Death of Major Peirson, *1782 - 83 by John Singleton Copley.*
The Samuel Courtauld Trust, The Courtauld Gallery, London (D.1952.RW.230)

Study for the fleeing women and child in The Death of Major Peirson, *1782 - 84 by John Singleton Copley.*
Photograph © 2012 Museum of Fine Arts, Boston (39.265b)

Studies for the The Death of Major Peirson, *1782 - 83 by John Singleton Copley.*
The Samuel Courtauld Trust, The Courtauld Gallery, London (D.1952.RW.1838)

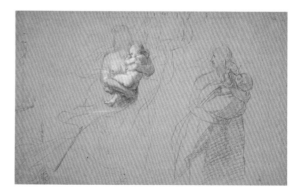

Study for the fleeing women and child in The Death of Major Peirson, *1782 - 84 by John Singleton Copley.*
Photograph © 2012 Museum of Fine Arts, Boston (39.266)

Study of fleeing women and child and boy with hat in The Death of Major Peirson, *1782 - 84 by John Singleton Copley.*
Photograph © 2012 Museum of Fine Arts, Boston (39.264)

Study for The Death of Major Peirson, Two Dead Figures, *1782 - 83 by John Singleton Copley.*
© 2011. Image copyright The Metropolitan Museum of Art/Art Resource/Scala, Florence (60.44.14 - recto)

Study for the officer and a wounded drummer in The Death of Major Peirson, *1782 - 84 by John Singleton Copley.*
Photograph © 2012 Museum of Fine Arts, Boston (39.262a)

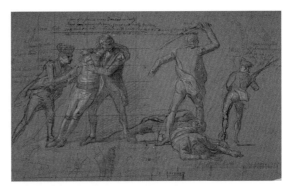

Study for The Death of Major Peirson, Dying French Officer Group and Other Figures, *1782 - 83 by John Singleton Copley.*
Photograph © 2012 Museum of Fine Arts, Boston (1939.270)

Study for The Death of Major Peirson, Group of Dying French Officers, *1782 - 83 by John Singleton Copley.*
© 2011. Image copyright The Metropolitan Museum of Art/Art Resource/ Scala, Florence (60.44.14 - verso)

Sketch for The Death of Major Peirson, *1782 - 84 by John Singleton Copley.*
Yale University Art Gallery, Lelia A and John Hill Morgan, B.A. 1893, LL.B. 1896, M.A. (Hon). 1929, Collection (1943.67)

The finished painting

The Death of Major Peirson is an image of tremendous visual power and high drama. The combination of intense colour, strong contrasts of light and dark and an action-packed composition generates a striking and arresting painting which portrayed the heat and confusion of battle. The strong diagonal lines of soldiers, buildings, flag masts and bayonets intensify the confusion of battle. The push of soldiers from left to right as they overwhelm the French is broken by the young child who runs forward, almost out of the picture and towards the audience. The painting had an immediate and powerful effect on its first viewers; *I never saw a painting more expressive than this. I looked upon it until I was faint; you can scarcely believe but you hear the groans of the sergeant, who is wounded, and holding the handkerchief to his side, whilst the blood streams over his hand.*[35]

One of the most striking things about *The Death of Major Peirson* is its size. It is big, some might say monumental, measuring roughly three metres by four metres when framed. It is difficult to convey this size in reproduction but suffice to say it would fit comfortably on the side of a double-decker bus. History paintings tended to be large, Copley's *The Death of the Earl of Chatham*, 1779 - 81 was a similar size. Copley did not need to paint a picture of this size for the purpose of making a print, which required a much smaller version to be made. In painting a picture of this magnitude, Copley was aiming for an overwhelming visual impact. The impact would help the audience experience the awe and terror inspired by the events of the picture and would help ensure that the audience remembered the experience of seeing the painting. This in turn would encourage sales of the print, but also helped cement Copley's reputation and success as London's foremost contemporary history painter.

Copley's manipulation of the painting's staging, lighting and figural arrangements had much in common with late eighteenth century theatrical productions. In the playhouse at the time, the stage often extended out into the audience, making them feel part of the action. The fleeing women and dying soldier at the bottom left corner echo this shaping of contemporary theatre, as they appear to extend out of the picture, increasing their proximity to the audience and making the viewer feel more part of the picture. Peirson's body falls towards us, his lifeless arm falling downwards, making the audience want to reach out towards him, like the injured sergeant in the left corner.

Nationalistic issues were often the subjects of theatrical productions, particularly wars with the French. A theatrical performance of the Battle of Jersey was announced a scant two weeks after the event, *This Evening will be presented a new Piece, called BRITONS TO ARMS; or WHO IS AFRAID IN JERSEY Ladies and Gentlemen instructed to ride on horseback,* and went on to elaborate *Besides the usual entertainments, there will be presented this evening, at Astley's Amphitheatre Riding school, Westminster Bridge, a representation of the French landing from their flat-bottom boats, and invading Jersey, together with the British troops attacking, defeating, and taking prisoners the French infantry. The whole of this piece is represented by shadows, which brings out a most pleasing effect; particularly in that part where the French and English are forming the line of battle, the English in columns beat the English grenadier march, and the French in divisions beat the French march; platoons are heard, also a continual fire from small-arms is kept up, till the French give way on all sides, and surrender themselves prisoners to the British troops.*[36] That the audience were instructed to ride on horseback suggests that eighteenth century theatrical audiences were encouraged and accustomed to becoming part of productions.

Through the characters in *The Death of Major Peirson*, Copley takes us through a carefully orchestrated series of emotions, from tranquillity and nobility through to terror and fear and then to anger and revenge. The central group of figures carrying Peirson's body are remarkably composed and serene, particularly the figures of Adjutant Harrison, Captain Corbet and Lieutenant Buchanan, (see page 52 for key). Ensign Rowan stares resolutely at the flag rather than at the chaos in front of him. Military training encouraged officers to be impassive and serene, particularly in trying circumstances when they would need to put emotion aside and get on with the job in hand. The most emotional military figure is the injured sergeant leaning against a company drum. Other than staunching the flow of his blood with a handkerchief, he concentrates solely on the figure of the dead Peirson, raising his arm as if to touch the fallen figure. His raised arm draws the viewer's eye to the central group, the main focus of the picture. Lieutenant Drysdale turns his head from the dead body and faces the same direction as Captain MacNeill and the figure called 'Major Peirson's black servant', known as Pompey, that is, towards the French forces, as if Lieutenant Drysdale like Pompey and Captain MacNeill seeks revenge for this loss. Captain Clephane has his back to the action and to Peirson as he points to his troops, directing their attack, his blood-soaked sword raised ready for action. From his experience as an artist, Copley would have well understood the military need for discipline and emotional detachment. In contrast to this military stoicism, the civilians in the painting are terrified and horrified by the events taking place around them. The civilian group is made of up a young child, his mother, a young baby and their nurse. This group may have been based on the perhaps apocryphal story told by a Monsieur Bisson and passed on to his daughter who was nurse to renowned Jersey beauty Lillie Langtry. In her diary *The Days I Knew*,

Lillie retells nurse Bisson's story of how Lillie's great-grandmother fled with her youthful family from the conflict, a scene witnessed by Monsieur Bisson.[37] The figure on the far right raises her arms in alarm and the other female figure gazes back at the battle scene, her mouth open in an expression of horror and disbelief. The child clutches on to her dress. Copley used his young son, John Singleton Copley Junior (later Baron Lyndhurst), as the model for this figure. The child gazes out at the audience, the only person to look out of the picture, directly engaging the audience in the painting so that the audience look at the scene through his innocent, uncorrupted eyes.[38]

Copley engages us, the viewer, by painting a single, instantaneous moment in time. Blood drips from Peirson's chest, our eyes following the drops to a pool

Detail of The Death of Major Peirson, *1783 by John Singleton Copley.*
© Tate, London 2011 (N00733)

forming on the ground, making us, the audience, feel that we are witness to the moment of his death. But the audience is given satisfaction as we are also engaged in the act of revenge, as we follow Captain MacNeill's finger and Pompey's gaze through the puff of smoke as he fires to the other side of the picture where the fallen figure of Baron de Rullecourt lies supported by his officers whose faces are filled with sadness. Above de Rullecourt the golden sculpture of George II stands unmoving and upright, representing a solid and resolute monarchy, with its enemies fallen at its feet. The statue stands alongside the Court House which has the Royal coat of arms above the door and a crown at the pinnacle of its tower, representing British justice and the rule of law. Justice has been served.

Exclusions and inclusions

Copley manipulated events in order to create a successful and memorable history painting. His experience as a history painter taught him that the public would accept a degree of artistic licence if this were compensated by a high level of accuracy on details, an approach which is still used by some of the best story makers today. An examination of his choice of which elements of the story to exclude and include helps illuminate what he considered to be the key messages of his painting and those that he judged best ignored.

Copley's artistic licence stretched to downplaying the presence of the 78th Highlander Regiment at the Battle. Both the 78th Highlanders and the 95th Regiments entered the Market Square (now the Royal Square),[39] but in Copley's painting the Highlanders' presence is indicated only by a dead Highlander lying alongside a bonnet on the floor and two figures in the background on the right, firing on the French. The majority of the 78th Highland Regiment is shown descending on the enemy from the hill of Mont de la Ville above the Market Square. The Highlanders wore distinctive national dress - a kilt, diced hose, red jacket and a dark blue bonnet with a chequered band and black feathers. The Highlanders were excluded from the painting for political reasons. The union between Scotland and England was fairly new having been formed in 1707 and there was still some antipathy and suspicion on both sides. The 78th Highlanders Regiment was made up of members of the Macrae clan who were loyal to Lord Seaforth. They later became known as the Seaforth Highlanders. In 1778 they were billeted at Edinburgh Castle. When ordered to embark to Jersey they rebelled for three days, believing they were being sold to the East India Company.[40] The Scottish Highlanders were replaced in the battle scene by English Grenadiers from the 95th Regiment who wore long scarlet jackets, white breeches and high bearskin hats, an appropriately English uniform for the English victory required by the English audience which Copley anticipated would be the most likely

Details of Highlanders in The Death of Major Peirson, *1783 by John Singleton Copley.*
© Tate, London 2011 (N00733)

to view the painting and buy a print. He did not wish to dilute this message by representing the distinctly and recognisably Scottish as having taken part. The Highlanders' actions were patriotically mentioned in the Scottish newspapers, *Our loss is about 70 killed and wounded, many of whom are Highlanders, who behaved to admiration, making the attack on the town, and dislodging the French from the houses, in which they put many of them to the sword. Lieutenant Robertson of the Glasgow Regiment, with 40 grenadiers of that corps, attacked and routed a party of 120 of the French, killing 26, and wounding about 30; after which the rest laid down their arms.*[41] A report in another newspaper hints at some of the issues being encountered, *They write from Jersey, that the Highlanders had performed wonders in the late attack on the Island; and that it was in a great manner owing to their unexampled bravery that the militia were tempted to follow up the route which had recovered the country from its invaders.*

The noble defence made by the inhabitants of Jersey shews (sic) the utility of every person in Britain being trained to arms. In a particular manner the inhabitants of Scotland, now since the war is begun against the Dutch, should be able to repel any hostile attack. It is hoped the narrow and illiberal idea, that the people of Scotland ought not to be trusted with arms in their own defence, will now give place to a measure of so much utility and even necessity.[42] Perhaps in consolation for their visual exclusion, Copley specifically acknowledged the role of Highlanders in the brochure which accompanied the first exhibition of *The Death of Major Peirson, On the other side of the Picture are Women and Children flying with terror and distress from this scene of blood; near them a Highland Sergeant lays dead, and a party of Highlanders are seen attacking the Enemy, who are flying for refuge into the Court-house.*[43]

A notable and distinct presence in the melee is a black soldier dressed in an elaborate green uniform and plumed hat. The presence of a black person in one of his paintings is not without precedent as Copley had painted a black figure in *Watson and the Shark*. In painting at this time a black person often patronisingly signified loyalty and duty, as he does here. The question is whether a black person actually fought in the Battle or whether he has been used by Copley as a symbol and political tool. There is some evidence that there was a black person present at the Battle of Jersey. Peirson's father stated that Adjutant Harrison told him that his son's death was avenged by a Jersey militiaman and the black servant (known as Pompey) of Captain Christy (sic) of the 95th Regiment. *The Glasgow Herald* of Thursday January 18 to Thursday January 25, 1781, printed a copy of a letter written from Jersey on January 10, *Mr Clement Hemery, who fought the whole time near poor Major Peirson, as did Maitre Ph.Gallais, a tradesman in this town, who distinguished himself greatly; so likewise did a Negro servant of Capt. Christie, of the 95th Regiment.* There was a Captain Christie of the 95th Regiment who fought in the Battle, but he is not depicted in the painting. Coincidentally Copley used the black servant of James Christie of the auctioneering house in London as the model, a coincidence that further confuses the black figure's status and role. There is no record that Peirson had a servant, although he would have had a monetary allowance for one. Perhaps he borrowed Captain Christie's servant. In 1790 *The Yorkshire Gazette* reported that the black servant of Major Peirson had applied for poor relief, further proof of this person's existence, although again somewhat confused as to whether he was Captain Christie's or Major Peirson's servant. Significantly Copley painted Pompey in the uniform of the Royal Ethiopian Regiment.[44] As a Loyalist, Copley would likely have been aware of the existence of this Regiment, which was made up of Black Loyalists who joined British colonial forces during the American Revolutionary War. The British promised enslaved people their freedom if

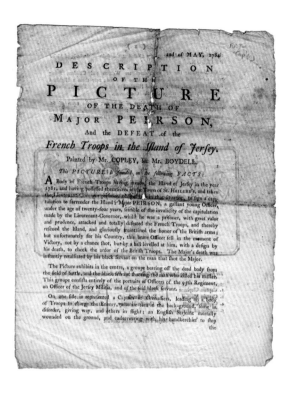

they escaped and formed into all black regiments, such as the Royal Ethiopians. Their uniforms were proudly embroidered with the slogan 'Liberty to Slaves', although this slogan does not feature in the painting. However, this regiment was never posted to Jersey and never fought in the battle. Copley's reasons for including this figure in this uniform could be manifold. Firstly, Copley was an American Loyalist who had fled Boston when things became too difficult for him there and he wished to spread his artistic wings, settling in London where he found a new and appreciative audience and prospered as an artist. By painting this Black Loyalist, Copley was associating himself with the Loyalist cause and supporting their aims. The French supported American forces both politically and militarily in the American War of Independence. In the painting, Pompey, a Black Loyalist shoots directly at the French, as his comrades were doing thousands of miles away, individualising and symbolising this stance. Also,

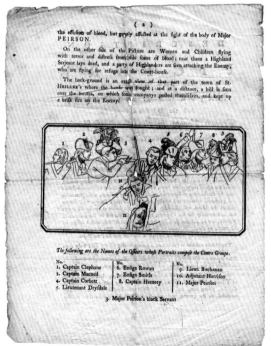

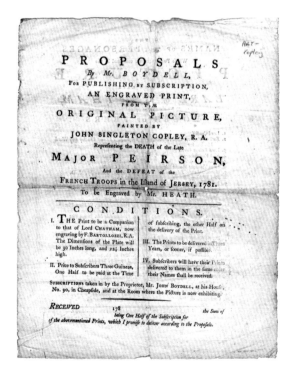

Subscription brochure for The Death of Major Peirson, *1783*
by John Singleton Copley published by John Boydell.
Courtesy of Lord Coutanche Library, Société Jersiaise

the inclusion of a black person reinforces Britain's role as a worldwide power. In the brochure for the painting, Copley advertised him as being Peirson's black servant avenging his death, suggesting the loyalty of a duty-bound servant. By associating Peirson with the black figure in this way, Copley personalised the revenge, making it a stronger and more empathetic emotion for the viewer.

A significant exclusion from the painting is the key figure of Lieutenant Governor Major Moyse Corbet. In accounts of the Battle and his court martial statement, Corbet stated that when the British attacked the French in the Market Square, Corbet left the court building with Baron de Rullecourt, who insisted that Corbet share the risk of action. A few minutes later Baron de Rullecourt was shot in the mouth.[45] In *The Death of Major Peirson* de Rullecourt lies in the arms of his fellow officers. Corbet was with de Rullecourt at the time he was shot but is not shown in the painting. By excluding him, Copley avoided having to tell the story of his capitulation, a story which could be interpreted as cowardice on the part of a British officer and which would not have fitted into the heroic theme of the painting.

The print

Copley and Boydell were keen to advertise the truth of the painting in the brochure which accompanied its exhibition. The brochure helped the viewer comprehend the painting's deeper meanings and gave them details of the events and people depicted.[46] Emotive and descriptive language was used, ensuring that the audience knew that Peirson was the hero and establishing the roles played by other characters.

DESCRIPTION OF THE PICTURE OF THE DEATH OF MAJOR PEIRSON And the DEFEAT of the French Troops in the Island of Jersey Painted by Mr.COPLEY, for Mr BOYDELL. This PICTURE is founded on the following FACTS: A Body of French Troops having invaded the Island of Jersey in the year of 1781, and having possessed themselves of the Town of St.Heiller's, and taken the Lieutenant Governor prisoner, obliged him in that situation, to sign a capitulation to surrender the Island; Major PEIRSON, a gallant young Officer, under the age of twenty-four years, sensible of the invalidity of the capitulation made by the Lieutenant-Governor, whilst he was a prisoner, with great valor and prudence, attacked and totally defeated the French Troops, and thereby rescued the Island, and gloriously maintained the honor of the British arms; but unfortunately for his Country, this brave Officer fell in the moment of Victory, not by a chance shot, but by a bullet levelled at him, with a design by his death, to check the ardour of the British Troops. The Major's death was instantly retaliated by his black servant on the man that shot the Major.

The Picture exhibits in the centre, a groupe bearing off the dead body from the field of battle, and the black servant shooting the man who killed his master. This groupe consists entirely of the portraits of Officers of the 95th Regiment, an Officer of the Jersey Militia, and of the said black servant.

On one side is represented a Captain of Grenadiers, leading on a body of Troops to charge the Enemy, who are seen in the back-ground, some in disorder, giving way, and others in flight; an English Sergeant mortally wounded on the ground, and endeavouring with his handkerchief to stop the effusion of blood, but greatly affected at the sight of the body of Major PEIRSON.

On the other side of the Picture are Women and Children flying with terror and distress from this scene of blood; near them a Highland Serjeant lays dead, and a party of Highlanders are seen attacking the Enemy, who are flying to refuge into the Court-house.

The back-ground is an exact view of that part of the town of St. HEILLER'S where the battle was fought; and at a distance, a hill is seen over the houses, on which some companys posted themselves, and kept up a brisk fire on the Enemy.

The brochure included a key giving the names and ranks of officers whose portraits comprised the central group. It also advertised the print of the painting and encouraged viewers to subscribe.

The life of *The Death of Major Peirson*

Although history painting was the most esteemed subject for artists, it was not profitable. There was a limited market for their sale as history paintings tended to be large and therefore expensive canvases, often representing several years of an artist's output. Copley's main income was from painting portraits but he made his reputation through history painting. Copley and entrepreneur John Boydell financed history painting by exhibiting and making prints. This bordered on a level of commercialism frowned upon by the Royal Academy, which preached that art's purpose was to educate, not for commercial gain. The Academy

believed that artists should not sully their God-given talent by tainting it with the offensive odour of money.

For the first exhibition of *The Death of Major Peirson*, Copley rented the Great Room at Spring Gardens in Haymarket, a popular venue for arts events. He charged an entrance fee of one shilling. *The Morning Post and Daily Advertiser* of Thursday May 13, 1784 advertised the show thus, *The picture painting for Mr. Alderman Boydell, Mr.Copley having almost compleated (sic), of the death of Major Peirson, and the defeat of the French troops in the Island of Jersey, most respectfully informs the public, that he intends to exhibit the said picture next week, in the Great Room in the Hay-market, No.28.* The following week the newspaper elaborated *EXHIBITION MR COPLEY most respectfully informs the Public, that the Picture which he has painted for Mr. Alderman Boydell, of the death of Major Peirson, and the defeat of the French troops in the Island of Jersey in the year 1781…will be exhibited on next Saturday morning, the 22nd May, in the Great Room in the Hay-market, No.28, where will be delivered an Explanation of the Picture, with the names of the officers whose portraits are contained within it: also Mr. Alderman Boydell's proposals for publishing a print from the said picture.*
Mr. Copley's Picture of the late Earl of Chatham, and the House of Peers, will be placed in the same Great Room, for the fascination of those who have not seen it.
The Room will be open on Saturday morning, and at eight o'clock in the morning until evening of the succeeding days, except Sundays.
Admittance One Shilling each person: The Explanation gratis.[47]

Straight after the Haymarket show the painting was moved to John Boydell's gallery-cum-shop at 90 Cheapside, then a centre for London's print selling establishments, where visitors could see not only works of art that Boydell had commissioned, but also

Frame design for The Death of Major Peirson *by Robert Adam. Courtesy of the Trustees of Sir John Soane's Museum.*
Photo: Ardon Bar-Hama

The Death of Major Peirson *after John Singleton Copley by James Heath. Engraving published by J and J Boydell, 1796.*
Jersey Heritage/Société Jersiaise Collection

other examples of prints commissioned by Boydell. The frame of the picture also acted as an advert for the print. Designed by Neoclassical architect Robert Adam, it was ornamented with carved cannons, weapons, British flags, bows, swags which resembled the edging on theatre curtains, a portrait of Copley by American artist Gilbert Stuart and portraits of James Heath, engraver of the picture, and Josiah Boydell, draftsman for the print.[48]

According to a 1789 newspaper report, the manufacture of the print of *The Death of Major Peirson* seemed to be progressing well, *HEATH'S companion to it, THE DEATH OF MAJOR PEIRSON, is in great forwardness;-*

the aquafortis proof is equal, if not superior, to any of the English School, and adds greatly to the already well-earned reputation of this distinguished Artist.[49] However the final, long-awaited print was not ready until 1796, when its price had risen to four guineas.

The original painting of *The Death of Major Peirson* remained in the ownership of John Boydell, as he originally commissioned the painting, and it appears that he kept it on display in his shop. In 1804, Boydell needed to liquidise some of his assets in order to invest in a project he was working on which was to commission British artists to paint Shakespeare's plays.[50] Boydell applied to Parliament to dispose of his

Plan of the Shakespeare Lottery.
© *Victoria and Albert Museum, London*

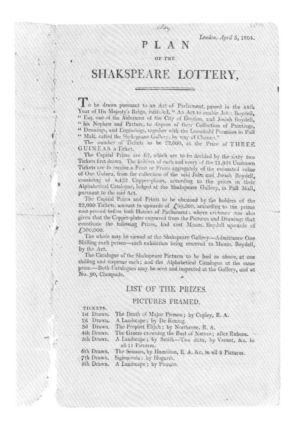

property by lottery. The first prize in this lottery was to be *The Death of Major Peirson*. Twenty-two thousand tickets were sold at a price of three guineas each.[51] The lucky winner was a Mr Tassie who sold his prize by auction, when it was purchased back by Boydell. Boydell put the painting up for auction again in 1805, but it remained unsold and Copley bought it back from Boydell. Copley probably received some financial help for this purchase from his son who was embarking on a career in the law. By this time Copley was struggling financially. Upon Copley's death in September 1815, his estate passed to his son, John Singleton Copley Junior, who had modelled for the figure of the fleeing child. In 1827 John Singleton Copley Junior became Baron Lyndhurst and was three times Lord Chancellor of

England. He died in 1864 and his paintings were put up for sale by Christie's. The States of Jersey decided to bid for the painting and set aside £1,000 for this purpose. Bailiff John Hammond was dispatched to London to undertake the bidding. Unfortunately he was outbid by Sir Charles Eastlake, Keeper of the National Gallery, who paid £1,600. The painting remained on display at either the National Gallery or Tate Gallery until it was permanently transferred to the Tate Gallery in 1957.

The States of Jersey were hugely disappointed that they had not set aside enough money to purchase *The Death of Major Peirson*, nor had States Members had the foresight to purchase it at earlier auctions. At the suggestion of the President of the Royal Academy a full-size copy of the painting was made by William Holyoake (1834 - 94). He was given permission to paint in the National Gallery in April 1866 and by the end of August the copy was finished and delivered to Jersey.[52] Whilst the copy is a very good and well painted reproduction, Holyoake was copying a painting which was over 70 years old and had spent much of its life in a no-doubt nicotine filled house, causing it to discolour. Holyoake's copy therefore lacks the vivacity of colouring present in the original.

The Death of Major Peirson continues to be encountered regularly in some form or another by people in Jersey. It has been replicated countless times and in a variety of ways. It has been printed on commemorative ceramics and has appeared on Jersey stamps and money. Objects owned by Major Peirson are revered for their association with this hero. The Battle has inspired countless poems and is usually marked on the anniversary in some way.

The main success of John Singleton Copley's career was to fashion contemporary history painting into a publicly and critically acceptable art form. *The Death of Major Peirson* marks the zenith of his career. By the time *The Death of Major Peirson* was complete in 1784, the American War of Independence was over. The painting provided a much-needed reminder of British military prowess and appealed to British patriotic fervour.

It captured the spirit of the moment but was such a powerful portrayal of sacrifice and heroism that it remains the embodiment of a war painting - full of action, narrative, nobility, stoicism and enduring patriotism. For many Islanders it reminds us of the efforts made by others throughout history to maintain our independence, reiterate our loyalty to the Crown and preserve our way of life.

The artist

John Singleton Copley (1738 - 1815) was an American artist, born in Boston, Massachusetts. In his youth he lived with his widowed mother over a tobacco shop she ran on Long Wharf, Boston, a bustling port. No doubt the young Copley would have encountered travellers from all over the world. His mother remarried Peter Pelham, a mezzotint scraper trained in England who made many portraits of members of Boston society. Pelham encouraged the young Copley in his efforts to teach himself to paint.[53]

Copley sent his first painting to London in 1766, a portrait of his half-brother Henry Pelham entitled *The Boy with a Flying Squirrel,* 1765. This portrait was well received. Copley continued to paint portraits and his reputation steadily grew. In 1768 he painted Paul Revere, the son of a Huguenot silversmith who is best known for his legendary midnight ride to alert the Colonial militia of a British invasion before the

Battles of Lexington and Concord. Copley's works of this period are characterised by great realism and attention to detail and were painted in a tight, linear style. Copley struggled with what he saw as the prevailing view in American society that artists were artisans rather than artists. Like many others, he was keen to elevate the social status of artists from that of a skilled worker to a gentleman using his God-given talent. This desire was in contrast to the plans of many members of the American Academy of Fine Arts who wished to encourage a 'national' art form, characterised by simplicity, directness and close attention to detail as opposed to the refinement and artificiality of European art.[54] Whilst painting for a colonial audience, Copley gave his clients what they wanted, which was, in general, an opportunity to display their often newly acquired material wealth. However, to the European audience this was regarded as commercial and vulgar.[55] Copley was later criticised by the American audience for abandoning his 'national' style. Whatever the opinions of others, Copley felt it was time to try something new. Largely self-taught, Copley was a successful artist in his native Boston. He achieved this success through a combination of hard work, intelligence, ambition, natural talent and the ability to give his clients what they wanted. However, if he was to grow and develop as an artist and explore new subject matter, he needed to move on to a new audience, find new inspiration and clients with different ideas of what was considered fine art.

The political and economic situation in Boston was becoming increasingly turbulent, another reason for Copley to move away. He and his family were committed Loyalists. He even had to ward off an angry mob that stormed his house demanding to know the whereabouts of Colonel George Watson, a Loyalist activist.[56] Copley's father-in-law, Richard Clarke, was the merchant to whom the tea that provoked the Boston Tea Party was consigned. Copley judged that the time was right to relocate. In June 1774 he sailed for England, staying only a short while before travelling to Paris and Rome. He left his wife Susanna (1745 - 1836, married 1769) and three children behind in Boston (Elizabeth 1770 - 1866, John Singleton Copley Junior 1772 - 1863 and Mary 1773 - 1868) until they were reunited in England in October 1775. Copley showed his first work at the Royal Academy in 1776 and was elected an associate member the same year. He continued to show at the Royal Academy right up to 1812. He began his move towards becoming a history painter by copying historical compositions, many of which he had seen during his travels from Paris to Rome. He continued to finance and establish himself as part of London society by painting portraits. In 1777 he showed a portrait of his family at the Royal Academy, advertising his ability as a portrait artist. He was greatly influenced as a history painter by his friendship with fellow American painter Benjamin West (1738 - 1820), historical painter to King George III and the second President of the Royal Academy (1792 - 1820). Copley was elected a Royal Academician (RA) in 1779 following the showing of his work *Watson and the Shark*, 1778, a contemporary history painting which depicts the dramatic rescue of 14-year-old Brook Watson from a shark attack in Havana harbour in Cuba in 1749, when Watson had his lower leg bitten off by a shark. Copley's next history painting depicted the dramatic collapse of the Earl of Chatham in the House of Lords. In this picture Copley painted individual portraits of members of the House of Lords and the painting is a testament to his desire to ensure that his history paintings were accurate on detail, in this case with portraits which closely resembled their sitters, wearing the correct robes and accoutrements. With *Watson and the Shark* and *The Death of the Earl of Chatham*, 1779 - 81, Copley

established himself as a leading history painter, but it was with *The Death of Major Peirson* that his career was to reach its public and critical peak. His reputation built to such an extent that his next work, *The Siege of Gibraltar*, 1783 - 91 was a direct commission from the Corporation of London.[57] This painting commemorated the British military victory in Gibraltar when the Spanish tried to retake the Rock.

Religious paintings and portraits dominated Copley's later work and his submissions to the Royal Academy. He struggled to maintain the momentum created by his history paintings of the 1770s to 1790s. It required tremendous financial commitment, as well as mental and physical strength to take on usually large and intricately detailed pieces. Increasingly Copley found that many of his history and religious paintings remained unsold. He was strained financially and even found himself in the embarrassing position of having to take loans from his son, John Singleton Copley Junior, which often remained unpaid. Copley died on 9 September 1815.

The Death of Major Peirson and war art

War art can be a record, a piece of reportage which realistically captures a scene, a piece of propaganda created to inspire loyalty and action from the viewer, or it can be a piece of artistic interpretation which attempts to portray the emotional impact of a momentous event. Rolling news reports and internet coverage have brought war into our living rooms and workplaces. Amongst the opposing sides in a war there is an awareness of the power of the media and the need to control, and if possible to manipulate, the presentation of war. This need to control and manipulate is no different for pre-television and internet war reporting. War art has existed for many centuries and is common to many nations. It is a way that countries help build the idea of nationhood. As war is global so is war art. *Trajan's Column*, c.100 AD, *The Bayeux Tapestry*, c.1070, Paolo Uccello's *Battle of San Romano*, c.1438 - 1440, Francisco Goya's *The Disasters of War*, 1810 - 1820, Pablo Picasso's *Guernica*, 1937 - these great masterpieces have been spawned by the brutality and nationalism of war. But war art is wider than these exalted representations, it is also war memorials, propaganda posters and photographs.

The term 'war art' is relatively new and at the time Copley was painting such pictures were known as 'battle-pieces'. In the eighteenth century, 'battle-pieces'[58] tended to be either heroic portraits or pictures of a battle. Astutely, Copley combined the two in *The Death of Major Peirson*. The heroic portrait implies prestige and justified military engagements. The battle painting told the nation about its achievements and encouraged a sense of national identity.[59] This was disseminated to the public through exhibiting the works and making them into prints set at a price which was affordable, at least to the middle classes.

Copley's skill as an artist was to combine records and facts about the Battle with his artistic interpretation of the event, creating a painting which provoked an emotional reaction to the Battle and the death of Major Peirson. Copley painted *The Death of Major Peirson* at a time when images of battles were like tributes that celebrated heroism. Churches were filled with memorials to wars and individuals, becoming mausoleums of centuries of human conflict. Patriotic hymns were often battle cries calling young men to arms. This was a time when Britain was transforming itself from a middle-sized European country into a colonial power, ruling the largest empire the world had

ever seen. War art often reflected this atmosphere of military might and success and acted as propaganda for the aims of this outlook. It provided heroes at a time when the nation needed them. Benjamin West's painting *The Death of General Wolfe* (see page 41) was one of the most reproduced paintings of the eighteenth century, decorating Georgian mansions, town houses and cottages. Throughout the nineteenth century artists continued to paint battle scenes in a highly romantic, celebratory and idealistic way.

It was as a reaction to the brutality and carnage of World War One that some artists and poets began to question the purpose of war and artists and poets challenged the view that art was about victory and glory. New battlefield technology and armaments made this a different kind of war, one which was dynamic and explosive, bringing unprecedented destruction to people and land. The British Government recognised the propagandist power of art and in 1916 set up a scheme to commission artists to paint their experiences. The intention was to provide eyewitness images which could illustrate propaganda. However, many artists abandoned any semblance of heroism and bravery and started to show war as a hellish arena of misery and death. The Ministry of

Paths of Glory, 1917 by C R W Nevinson.
© *crown copyright IWM art 518*

Raising the Flag on Iwo-Jima, *1945 by Joe Rosenthal/AP.*

Information censored some of their paintings. C R W Nevinson's painting of dead Tommies *Paths of Glory*, 1917 was censored so he took the provocative step of exhibiting it with a 'censored' banner stuck crudely across it.

During the Second World War artists once again became reporters from the front line, this time marshalled by the Director of the National Gallery, Kenneth Clark who used the National Gallery as the venue for showing war art by modern artists. Attendances soared and art acted as a unifying force drawing people together as witnesses to other people's experiences of war. Art was used as a morale booster, showing all sorts of people doing their bit. One of the most famous images of the Second World War is a photograph taken by an American Associated Press reporter, Joe Rosenthal. The photograph entitled *Raising the Flag on Iwo Jima* depicts a group of marines raising the American flag on the Japanese island of Iwo Jima during a hard-fought battle. The photograph records the second flag raising on the mountain, the first having been a much smaller flag and an occasion missed by the photographer. Much controversy has surrounded this photograph, with stories of it being

set up for the camera. These stories have been denied by Rosenthal but have continued to circulate. The impact of the photograph was huge. The American nation saw it as a potent symbol of victory, particularly as some of the marines raising the flag later died in battle. It won a Pulitzer Prize in 1945, was used as the basis for the United States Marine Corps War Memorial and put on a US postage stamp. In recognition of the contribution Rosenthal's photograph had made to the war effort, Rosenthal was posthumously awarded the Distinguished Public Service Medal by the Marine Corps. The citation referred to his photograph that *immortalised the American Fighting Spirit during World War II and became an everlasting symbol of service and sacrifice, transcending art and ages.*[60] Whether this iconic photograph is an accurate record of a wartime event or an artificially constructed scene made to generate positive publicity around this harrowing event, the US government was swift and efficient in taking advantage of the propaganda generated by the image.

The truthfulness of war art can and should be questioned. It is influenced by issues of power and nationhood and the dissemination of these ideas. It is often difficult to accept that paintings like *The Death of Major Peirson* are not eyewitness accounts but the artist's interpretation of an event designed to generate a reaction from the audience. The most successful war art - be it a romantic evocation, an accurate representation or a piece of propaganda - acts as a permanent commemoration that will provoke and move generations to come. The main message of *The Death of Major Peirson* is that the true cost of war is the price paid by the individual for the benefit of others. Peirson is the dutiful soldier prepared to make the ultimate sacrifice, a hero for a society which needed, and still needs, heroes.

Endnotes

1. Admiral Arbuthnot writing from on board his ship states that the French invasion fleet numbered five ships of war, several bomb vessels and 50 boats and that they were landing men at 11 o'clock. An Edinburgh newspaper, *The Caledonian Mercury*, reported that the French fleet was made up of five frigates, four other vessels and a number of boats.

2. Letter from Corbet to Lord Weymouth, 1 May, 1779.

3. *The London Gazette* 9 January 1781, reported in *Morning Herald* of 10 January, 1781.

4. The other five companies of the 78th and 83rd Regiments were stationed in Guernsey along with all of the 96th Regiment of Foot.

5. When the French invaded Jersey, Peirson as a major was the senior British army officer on the Island after the Lieutenant Governor. The senior officers of both the 78th Foot and the 83rd Foot were captains.

6. The Engineers changed to a blue coat in 1782.

7. The grenadier company wore tall black bearskin caps, whilst the Light infantry company would have worn some form of light cap and short spatterdashes rather than gaiters. It was common practice for Grenadiers in the field to abandon their bearskin caps in favour of the more practical cocked hat.

8. In 1831 when they were given the designation Royal Jersey Militia all five regiments adopted the blue facings.

9. It is worth noting that commissions could be bought and sold in Britain's eighteenth century army.

10. Letter from Mons. d'Herville published in the *Courrier de l'Europe*, 6 March, 1781.

11. Robert Beatson, *Naval and Military Memoirs of Great Britain 1727 - 1783*, Vol 5 London 1804.

12. Captain Mulcaster's letter to Lord Amherst, 7 Jan 1781.

13. Alexander Glinn, John Hunter, William McCulloch, Alexander McKechney, James Reid, Robert Walker and John Wilson.

14. Lieutenants Godfray and Aubin.

15. Ensign Poignant.

16. Philippe Cabot and Jean Le Gros.

17. Rev. Le Couteur's letter, 12 January, 1781.

18. There is much about Hemery's testimony that needs to be reassessed. His whereabouts on the morning of the battle needs more attention as newspaper reports in the immediate aftermath give him credit for actually being involved with the action at Platte Rocque although this may be a misunderstanding and Captain Clement Hemery should actually read Reverend Le Couteur.

19. *Newcastle Courant* Saturday January 20, 1781.

20. Gentlemen volunteers served in the ranks as a common soldier but, because of their social status, messed with the officers. It was a way for gentlemen, lacking influence, who could not afford to purchase a commission to gain experience while waiting for an ensign's position to become available.

21. *The Edinburgh Advertiser* 12 to 16 January, 1781.

22. *The Edinburgh Evening Courant* 15 January, 1781.

23. *The Glasgow Mercury* Thursday 11 January to Thursday 18 January, 1781.

24. *The Edinburgh Evening Courant* 22 January, 1781.

25. *The Glasgow Mercury* Thursday 11 January to Thursday 18 January, 1781.

26. *The Middlesex Journal and Evening Post* 13 January to 16 January, 1781.

27. *The Edinburgh Evening Courant* 22 January, 1781.

28. *The Edinburgh Evening Courant* Wednesday 24 January, 1781 and *The Gazetteer and New Daily Advertiser* Friday 19 January, 1781.

29. *The London Chronicle* Tuesday 1 May to Thursday 3 May, 1781.

30. *The Edinburgh Advertiser* 4 May to 8 May, 1781.

31. Richard H Saunders 'Genius and Glory: John Singleton Copley's "The Death of Major Peirson"' in *American Art Journal*, Vol.22, No.3 (Autumn, 1990), p.4 to 39, p.14.

32. Philip Stevens *Dictionary of Painters of the Channel Islands*, JAB publishing, Jersey, 2002.

33. Saunders p.14.

34. Emily Ballew Neff *John Singleton Copley in England* Merrell Holberton, London, 1995, p.79.

35. Neff, p.83.

[36] *The Gazeteer and the New Daily Advertiser* Tuesday 23 January, 1781.

[37] Lillie Langtry *The Days I Knew* Redberry Press 1989.

[38] Neff, p.90.

[39] Saunders, p.30.

[40] Saunders, p.31.

[41] *The Glasgow Mercury* Thursday 11 January to Thursday 18 January, 1781.

[42] *The Edinburgh Evening Courant* Wednesday 17 January, 1781.

[43] *Description of the Picture of the Death of Major Peirson and the Defeat of the French Troops in the Island of Jersey*, London, 22 May, 1784.

[44] 'Black Loyalist in New Brunswick' in www.atlanticportal. hil.unb.ca/acva/blackloyalists/en/ and 'Lord Dunmore and the Ethiopian Regiment' by Pam Forsythe, Sam Houston State University, www.studythepast.com/ history571/.

[45] *The Glasgow Mercury* Thursday 11 January to Thursday 18 January, 1781.

[46] Neff, p.86.

[47] *The Morning Post and Daily Advertiser* Thursday 20 May, 1784.

[48] Neff, p.67.

[49] *The Morning Post and Daily Advertiser* Saturday 21 February, 1789.

[50] Marguerite Syvret *The Death of Major Peirson: the story of the picture and its painters* Jersey, 1988, p.7.

[51] Syvret, p.7.

[52] Letter to Ralph N Wornum, Keeper of the National Gallery from William Holyoake with a footnote from Ralph Wornum agreeing to the request and announcement in *Nouvelle Chronique de Jersey*, mercredi 29 aôut, 1866 both reproduced in Syvret.

[53] Syvret, p.1.

[54] Neff, p.18.

[55] Neff, p.21.

[56] Saunders, p.7.

[57] Neff, p.41.

[58] Laura Brandon *Art & War*, I B Tauris, New York, 2007 p.2.

[59] Brandon, p.28.

[60] Odom, Sgt. Christine C. 17 Sept, 2006 'Marine Corps awards Joe Rosenthal distinguished Public Service Medal' *Marine Corps News*.